Western USA

Claude Hervé-Bazin

JPM G̃uides

Contents

- The American West — 3
- Flashback — 9
- California — 15
  - San Francisco — 15
  - Central Coast — 29
  - Sierra Nevada — 37
  - Los Angeles — 41
  - San Diego and the Desert — 49
- Las Vegas — 54
- The Wild West — 57
  - Utah — 57
  - Arizona — 63
  - New Mexico and Colorado — 79
- Cultural Notes — 90
- Shopping — 93
- Dining Out — 95
- Sports — 100
- The Hard Facts — 102
- Index — 112

Maps

USA 6–7, Las Vegas 110, San Diego 111

Fold-out map

Southwest USA, Los Angeles, San Francisco

The American West

Wide Open Spaces

In the American West, nature's wildest fantasies seem to have come true. Three states—California, Utah and Arizona—have the lion's share of the country's most spectacular sites and national parks. Americans are well known for boasting that everything about their country is bigger and better than everywhere else. But it must be admitted that here in the West, they may have a point—the forces of nature have worked in harmony to produce scenery that can be described only by a litany of superlatives. The deepest canyon, the highest waterfall, the steepest mountain walls and the most fantastically eroded rocks—you will find them all in the Grand Canyon, Monument Valley, Bryce Canyon and Yosemite National Park.

With its vast red deserts and stunning backdrop of sculptured mountains and towering cactus, the American West is a familiar image to everyone the world over, thanks mainly to cowboy films. This is a place where dreams and drama are intrinsic to the theatrical setting.

Long before its discovery by Europeans, the Indians of Utah bestowed on their beloved territory the poetic name of "land of frozen arches". The scenery will no doubt arouse the poet in you, too, when at the end of a long day of travel, over seemingly endless roads through an equally infinite landscape, the red, sinking sun appears to set the very stones on fire.

Native Americans

Inseparable from the surroundings, the unique culture of the American Indian has its roots in the Far West. The past and present of this region are intricately entwined with the story of its Indian nations. In Arizona and New Mexico, territories larger than several English counties put together are the exclusive domains of tribes such as the Navajo, the Hopi and the Apache, whose history has left traces all around.

Within its reservation, each nation enacts its own laws (in so far as there is no conflict with federal law) and, since recent times, teaches its own language. Native American culture is based on the sacred. If you take time to understand the significance of the Bison and Maize dances, or even the buttes and mesas of the landscape, your trip will take on a deeper meaning.

THE AMERICAN WEST

A Geography Lesson

Approximately equivalent in size to the whole of Europe, the United States covers several distinct geographical regions and different climatic zones. Dominating the entire western part of the country, the Rocky Mountains constitute the American sector of a range that stretches along the entire length of the continent, from Alaska to Tierra del Fuego. Formed as a result of tectonic movement, they are the setting for many volcanic phenomena: several sites in the West erupt in geysers (in Yellowstone National Park for example), hot springs or sulphurous vents.

The widest part of this long mountain chain is in the United States. Between the foothills of the Sierra Nevada in California and the eastern slopes of the true Rockies in Colorado, it spans almost 1,500 km (900 miles). In reality there are three parallel ranges running north to south. To the east, the Rockies stretch mainly through the states of Colorado, Wyoming, Idaho and Montana; further west, in California, the Sierra Nevada is prolonged towards the north by the Cascade Range. The Coastal Range is lower but nevertheless impressive, especially in those places where it plunges directly into the Pacific Ocean. The vegetation found here is alpine.

Between the Sierra Nevada and the Rocky Mountains, the crests give way to upland plateaux of semi-desert, several of which have been chiselled by fast-flowing rivers. In this way, over millions of years, the Colorado River formed the Grand Canyon. Plunging down to a depth of 1,600 m (5,250 ft), the sides of the canyon reveal layers of rock dating back nearly 2 billion years. The variegated stripes of schist, gneiss, sandstone and shale tell its history like the pages of a book.

Sheltered from any maritime influence by the Sierra Nevada, the region is extremely arid. Here the elements have sculpted the bare rock: wind and frost, heat and the burrowing roots of plants, all have churned it up and worn away the surface in nature's gradual and never-ending process of transformation. The vegetation is well adapted to conditions of drought, and, especially nearer to Mexico, is dominated by impressive giant cactus such as the saguaro and the organ pipe.

Vast geological depressions are scattered throughout this zone, from Utah's Great Salt Lake to California's Death Valley, the lowest point in the United States at 86 m (282 ft) below sea-level. Wildlife is abundant here: mountain goats, fallow-deer, wild sheep, coyotes, bears, pumas.

THE AMERICAN WEST

City Life

Europeans are usually taken aback by the sheer immensity of American cities. They spread out their tentacles over hundreds, sometimes thousands, of square miles. The population, strongly urban (80 per cent live in towns) and with a tradition of home-ownership, have greatly contributed to this outward expansion. The suburbs are the centre of life for most people, who commute daily between their homes and downtown, where most of the jobs are to be found.

The European idea of a town has no equivalent here, where streets are invariably laid out on a grid system, intersecting at right angles and identified by numbers and letters. The facilities that Europeans would expect to find when walking around their own town centres simply do not exist in the United States. While there are indeed interesting monuments to visit, the town centre is not a place one would choose for a casual stroll. Here the automobile is king. There are virtually no pedestrian zones, hardly any cosy little cafés or tea rooms to pop into, and very few shops other than big department stores.

Los Angeles

The City of Angels is larger than life in all respects—the very image of America. Its greater urban area covers an incredible 88,000 sq km (34,000 sq miles), spreading from the shores of the Pacific Ocean to the eastern suburbs, skirting the Mojave Desert.

While undeniably an economic and industrial metropolis, Los Angeles has become one of the most popular cities in the United States. The climate is almost always sunny and pleasantly warm; the "dream factory" of Hollywood, the beaches and palm trees give the place a magnetic appeal. In the eyes of most Americans, Los Angeles is primarily a fun city and a land of opportunity, where the American Dream is well within grasp. Hundreds of hopefuls arrive every day to seek the good life.

San Francisco

The "City on the Bay", on the other hand, seems like a town with its feet solidly planted on the ground. San Francisco's incomparable charm—at once old-fashioned and cosmopolitan—will make you fall in love at first sight. Built on 43 hills overlooking a bay open to the Pacific, it is quite simply stunning. Its steep streets lined with Victorian houses, its jolting trams, the views and the Golden Gate Bridge make it a place not to be missed. The San Franciscans love it. And not even the threat of an earthquake can persuade them to leave!

Flashback

Earliest Inhabitants

The first inhabitants of the American continent did not originate there. It is generally agreed that waves of immigration during the Neolithic period brought the earliest adventurous colonists by way of the Bering Strait some 15,000 to 20,000 years ago. The nomadic hunter-gatherers of Asia probably expanded to the east in pursuit of the mammoth during the last glacial era when a bridge of land existed between the continents. Little is known of their pattern of dispersion, but the entire continent was occupied when the first Europeans came.

In some areas, brilliant civilizations developed—the Maya, the Inca, the Aztec—but the vast size of North America led to very heterogeneous settlement and, in general, prevented the blossoming of great cultures. The first European explorers did not realise that more than 400 major tribal groups were already living here, with distinct languages and social organization. Most of the tribes lived in peace, some trading with each other, while others were continually at war.

The newcomers' simplified perception of the way of life of these so-called "savages" resulted in a long-lasting lack of understanding of their society. There were three main zones of development. The eastern tribes included the Iroquois, who were hunters and fishers. The Plains Indians, notably the Sioux, were buffalo hunters. The tribes of the Southwest included the nomadic Apache and Navajo, and the Pueblos, so-named by the Spanish because they were sedentary farmers. This fragmentation of the Amerindian population led to a lack of cohesion in their struggle against the white man who came to usurp their territory.

The Spanish West

He may have discovered the Americas, but Christopher Columbus never actually set foot on the land that now constitutes mainland United States. The first to explore the North American continent was a Spaniard, Ponce de Léon. Disembarking in Florida in 1513, he set off in search of the Fountain of Youth, which was mentioned in certain Indian traditions. Fifteen years later, another

In Tombstone, Arizona, waiting for the gunfight at O.K. Corral.

Spanish conquistador, Francisco Vázquez de Coronado left Mexico to venture further northwards. He was searching for an Eldorado, the seven legendary cities of Cibola, said to be roofed with gold, and he was the first European to set eyes on the landscapes of the American West. One of his lieutenants, García López de Cárdenas, reached the south rim of the Grand Canyon. Spain dominated the first conquest of the West and defended their territory jealously. Indian resistance was disorganized, and the tribes, less numerous than in the Plains and around the Great Lakes, could not put up much resistance.

In 1609, Santa Fe was made the capital of Spanish possessions in this part of the New World, but finding no riches there, the conquistadors soon became disenchanted and made little effort to exploit their gains. Instead, Spain turned to establishing missions to convert the indigenous populations. Led by the Jesuits, these proselytizing campaigners wielded the Bible and the musket with equal zeal, attempting to convert the Indians to Christianity and a sedentary lifestyle. Their violent methods were resisted here as elsewhere in America. In 1680 a major revolt erupted in New Mexico, which the Spanish army was unable to subdue for several years. Gradually, a network of military outposts spread out over the land until it reached California, hitherto uncolonized. At the end of the 18th century, during a second wave of colonization, 21 missions were set up at the instigation of the Franciscan Father Junípero Serra. San Diego was the first, followed later by Los Angeles and San Francisco, built along part of the Camino Real, or King's Highway, a trail that connected Mexico City to Santa Fe.

American Expansion

The 19th century saw a spectacular territorial expansion of the United States, which had shaken off British rule by successfully waging the American War of Independence between 1776 and 1781.

The notion of conquest was implicit in the Constitution, which provided for the creation of new states. In 1803, France under Bonaparte ceded Louisiana for a derisory sum, together with vast territories stretching as far north as Canada. Shortly afterwards, Jefferson organized an expedition into Spanish territory under the guise of a scientific mission. His two envoys reconnoitred the future Oregon Trail. In 1819, the American government purchased Florida from Spain. Around that time, 60,000 colonists, who had come by sea, were already settled in California, a possession of Mexico which became independent in 1821. The population pressure increased continually with the steady flow of European settlers coming to seek a good new life in a new land. Between 1830 and 1850, the number of immigrants doubled each year.

The "frontier" was pushed back daily, until it finally reached Mexican soil. In 1845, American colonists in Texas, another Mexican state, began to stir up trouble in order to encourage annexation by the United States. Inevitably, war broke out. Three years later, the vanquished Mexicans signed the Treaty of Guadalupe, ceding the enormous territory of California, New Mexico and Arizona to the Union. The Mormons, who had been hounded across the country, took this opportunity to settle in the harsh lands of Utah. Henceforth, from the Atlantic to the Pacific, the United States occupied the entire North American continent.

The Gold Rush

At the beginning of 1848, only a few days before Mexico ceded California to the United States, one James Wilson Marshall, a carpenter from New Jersey, discovered a few gold nuggets along the American River near Colona and handed them over to his boss, John Sutter. The news spread like wildfire, and before the month of August was out the nearby hills were covered with the tents and shacks of the first 4,000 miners. Gold was panned by the bucketful from the riverbed. Working back to the source, the miners progressively approached the mother lode which stretched for 200 km (125 miles) into the foothills of the Sierra Nevada.

The discovery of gold in California was destined to change the political and economic history of the United States of that era. The tales of fortunes made in mere moments drew hordes of immigrants from around the world, even though very few of them actually found gold and riches. The Gold Rush was on! Coming from the east, the fortune-seekers either sailed all the way around Cape Horn—which involved several months at sea—or took a short cut on foot across the isthmus of Panama. The more hardy characters chose to follow the overland route. In 1849, 40,000 arrived by sea, while the same number made the journey by land.

The extent of its gold reserves (some 2 billion dollars worth of gold were to be exploited) hastened the entry of California into the Union. It became a state in 1850. The Gold Rush reached its zenith in 1852.

> FLASHBACK

The number of immigrants continued to rise long afterwards, but exhaustion of the main seams, together with stricter governmental control, gradually curtailed mining until it stopped altogether in the 1930s.

The Iron Horse

To unify the country, the government opened up routes towards the West. The California Gold Rush had started the ball rolling in 1848. The 600-km (375-mile) Erie Canal, linking Lake Erie to the Hudson River, was inaugurated in 1853. By 1855, not long before the American Civil War broke out, the railroad stretched as far as Chicago, and then Missouri. The war largely bypassed the West, but the region had its own problems to contend with. Further development of the railways linking the west coast to Missouri (through private enterprise) provoked troubles with the Indians. Between 1870 and 1930, the tribes were forced to give up more than half their lands.

The Indian wars shook the entire country, and by the close of the 19th century the West was bathed in blood. The famous Pony Express, which carried the mail between Missouri and Sacramento in California, did so only at great risk. The Apache and Navajo were finally defeated in 1867 and forced to settle in reservations.

In 1869, the railway tracks finally met: henceforth the Iron Horse of the Union and the Central Pacific Railroad linked the Atlantic and Pacific coasts. In the euphoria that followed, several other

The buttes and mesas of Monument Valley in the heart of Navajo country — backdrop to just about every cowboy film.

cross-country lines were opened: from Los Angeles to Saint-Louis and then from Los Angeles to New Orleans. But every step in this development trampled further on Indian lands. By 1890, the native population of North America had been brought from 10 million down to only 250,000.

Depression and Boom

The 20th-century history of the West in general and California in particular is mainly marked by a spectacular population explosion. During the Depression, immigrants from all over the United States flocked here to find work, as unemployment was less severe than in other, more industrialized parts of the country. Southern California and Hollywood, symbols of the good life, especially attracted newcomers, though it didn't work out for them all, as documented in John Steinbeck's novel *The Grapes of Wrath*.

Agriculture in the fertile valleys enjoyed an unprecedented boom. With World War II and the installation of many industries in urban areas, the West became a major economic zone. Immigration continued, with the population doubling every 20 years.

From the 1950s onwards, a great number of scientists and intellectuals came down to the West Coast and settled, and its research institutes consequently grew in stature. The most important universities, taking their lead from Berkeley, developed into major centres of learning. In the 1970s, after the euphoria of hippies and flower power, San Francisco and its region became the focus of protest and counter-culture (especially in the Haight-Ashbury district). At the same time, the liberalization of moral conventions attracted a large homosexual community, which gradually converted San Francisco into America's gay capital.

Modern Times

Today, the vitality of the West is fired essentially by its colourful multi-ethnic character. As the meeting point of America and Asia, influences from around the globe are keenly felt here. Now, three centuries later, the Eldorado which the Spanish sought in vain is within everyone's grasp. Despite some inevitable problems, the West still exerts a strong pull, and its aura continues to fire the popular imagination at the dawn of the 21st century.

California

One American in eight lives in the Golden State, the richest in the land. If California were an independent country, it would be the sixth economic power in the world. Such astonishing success has only confirmed Californians in their belief that they are somehow different. Visitors will discover two distinct regions centred on San Francisco, liberal and intellectual and gateway to the mountainous north, and Los Angeles, sun-worshipping and hedonistic at the doors of the southern deserts. Like twins, they have their similarities, but they relish their differences jealously, each being proud of its heritage and outlook. All along the shore, the magnificent Pacific Ocean pounds its waves against the foothills of the Coastal Range.

SAN FRANCISCO
Golden Gate Bridge, The Hills, City Centre, The Islands, The Bay Area

Steep hills, cramped housing and the constant threat of earthquake have done nothing to diminish San Francisco's great universal appeal. Everybody's favourite city does, after all, enjoy remarkable beauty and an uncommon cosiness, nestled as it is in the hills around the bay. Where else is a bridge—the dramatic Golden Gate—a work of art? Where else are trams—those clanging, rattling cable cars—fondly considered a historic monument?

As for the hills, which are as steep as all those film chases led you to believe, they provide vantage points for spectacular views. And you'll soon discover that in perennially cool San Francisco, the nip in the air is invigorating rather than chilly, and even the fog rolling off the Pacific seems romantic, not damp at all.

Take a tram ride for a bird's-eye view of the bay and Alcatraz.

The population of San Francisco is made up of an amazing diversity of nationalities and races. The largest single ethnic group today is Chinese. This most urbane of all American cities provides the finer things of life in abundance: elegant shopping, a cuisine of renown and a lively nightlife that ranges from topless bars to classical ballet. It's an intellectual and cultural trend-setter, the cradle of beatniks and flower power, student revolution, hippies and hot tubs. No problem: tolerant San Franciscans respect all kinds of non-conformists.

The city's rich and racy past was forged in the middle of the 19th century when the Gold Rush offered opportunity for all who were daring enough to try their luck. It was tempered by the great earthquake of 1906 and subsequent fire that raged for three days, leaving a quarter of a million residents homeless. Another killer quake in 1989 was a reminder that the city is always vulnerable. But while they wait for "the big one" to strike, San Franciscans remain unabashedly in love with their town, enjoying its charms to the hilt. Their pervasive enthusiasm is hard to resist.

Golden Gate Bridge

The bridge over the entry to the bay has become the emblem of San Francisco. When completed, in 1937, it was the longest and highest single-span suspension bridge in the world. It measures 1,280 m (1,400 yd) in length, and its two pillars rise 200 m (656 ft) above the cold waters of the bay, where the current can sweep in and out at speeds reaching 100 kph (62 mph).

The bridge is not golden in colour (in fact the name refers to the bay that it straddles), but a deep burnt sienna or reddish brown, depending on the light. It took four years to build and now takes just as long to repaint—and as soon as the finishing touches are applied it's time to start all over again. In addition to its six traffic lanes, there are two wide sidewalks so that pedestrians can admire the incomparable view of the city. Crossing the bridge on foot qualifies as something of an urban adventure. The roadway sways beneath your feet and the lampposts rattle as the wind whistles through the swooping cables.

At each end there's a viewing area. The Presidio, on the south side, was built by the Spanish in 1776, and includes public gardens where the citizens like to stroll or jog. Northwest of the bridge, the rugged heights of

The Golden Gate is not the bridge, but the entrance to San Francisco Bay.

Marin Headlands are part of the Golden Gate National Recreation Area.

Marina District

Heading towards the city centre, by way of a mile-long promenade, you pass through the Marina District, home to the Palace of Fine Arts, the last vestige of the 1915 Panama-Pacific Exhibition, which marked the opening of the Panama Canal. The child-friendly educational displays of the Exploratorium are an excellent introduction to the world of science. Marina is overlooked by the fashionable Pacific Heights district, one of the worst hit by the 1906 earthquake. Some beautiful old houses survived nonetheless, of which only the Haas-Lilienthal is open to the public.

Fisherman's Wharf

Past Fort Mason park, site of the Mexican Museum, the Craft and Folk Art Museum and others, is Marina Green, where the breakwater incorporates old cemetery headstones. The yacht harbour is at the end of the promenade. Old vessels of the San Francisco Maritime National Historical Park ride at anchor here. The design of the nearby Maritime Museum resembles that of a ferry.

Fisherman's Wharf is well frequented by tourists, who come to shop or to dine out in the many seafood restaurants. The quays are lined with tempting stalls offering an array of fresh crab and shrimp. A disused fruit-canning factory, the Cannery, and a chocolate factory in Ghirardelli Square have been converted into shopping centres. On Pier 39 (Embarcadero and Beach St), the Aquarium of the Bay has glass tunnels enabling you to view the bay's marine life.

The Hills

The best known of the hills are Nob, Telegraph and Russian. They were the original residential areas, featuring frequently in American literature, particularly in the works of Mark Twain. Implanted with pastel-coloured Victorian villas that were once the summer residences of the well-to-do, this area represents the quintessence of old San Francisco. The best way to get there is to hop on one of the cable cars which have been trundling up and down the slopes since 1873. Their means of locomotion could hardly be simpler: below the ground an endless cable moves at a constant 15 kph (9 mph), and the driver operates a clamp which grips the cable to haul the tram forward and releases it to stop.

Russian Hill

Named after an old trappers' cemetery, Russian Hill is still predominantly residential and studded with smart highrise apartment buildings. With little lanes opening onto esplanades overlooking the city and its windows hanging over the bay, it's an area of great charm and home to many writers. For a truly delirious experience, try walking down Lombard Street, called "the crookedest street in the world". Between Hyde and Leavenworth, it includes eight hairpin bends, whose only function is to amuse. Nearby Filbert Street claims to be the world's steepest street open to traffic—with a startling gradient of 31.5 per cent (almost 1 in 3).

Nob Hill

Close to Russian Hill, Nob Hill used to be the most desirable address in town. Here the nabobs or "nobs" lived in monumental Victorian residences. But all the houses were wiped out in the 1906 earthquake and subsequent fire, except for the imposing brownstone of James Flood, now the highly exclusive gentlemen-only Pacific Union Club. The hill boasts two of San Francisco's most gracious old hotels, the Fairmont and the Mark Hopkins, both of which have a panoramic bar with uninterrupted views over the city.

On the corner of Washington and Mason streets, the Cable Car Museum, situated at the nerve centre of San Francisco's famous tram system, is well worth a visit. It occupies the winding house for the cables controlling the cars, and you can see them at work in an underground viewing room.

Telegraph Hill

At the top of Telegraph Hill, the old lookout post for incoming ships, stands the surprising Coit Tower, shaped like a fire hose: it was erected in the 1930s by a rich heiress in tribute to the heroism of the city's firemen. The inside is decorated with paintings by local artists in the Social-Realism style of the Mexican painter Diego Rivera, depicting California life in the Great Depression.

City Centre

At the heart of San Francisco, dozens of department stores and luxury boutiques grace Union Square. A major crossroads, it is the place to see all kinds of characters: soap-box orators, street musicians, tramps, chess-players and picnickers. A few minutes' walk away, the Chinatown Gate opens onto the Chinese district.

Chinatown

Built in 1969 as a gift from Taiwan to the San Franciscan Chinese community, the gate marks the southern boundary of the Dai Fo, or "great town" as its inhabitants call the Chinese district. It is

a labyrinth of tiny shops, street stalls, narrow lanes and hidden courtyards. Pagodas turn out to be banks; lampposts look like Chinese lanterns. The "ghetto" days, when the Asian workforce was scarcely tolerated, are long gone, and today Chinatown has prospered and become the biggest Chinese community outside Asia. Grant Avenue runs through the middle and most of the shops catering to tourists are found here. On Stockton Street, souvenir sellers cede the place to greengrocers, whose produce is as exotic and varied as in the markets of Hong Kong or Canton. There are hundreds of restaurants serving delicious dishes at low prices. The local speciality is *dim sum*, a typical Cantonese snack, consisting of a variety of steamed or fried dumplings stuffed with meat, shrimp or vegetables.

At 965 Clay Street, the Chinese Historical Society of America Museum displays old photos recalling the Chinese era in the American West.

North Beach

Chinatown encroaches slightly upon North Beach, the centre of the 150,000-strong Italian community, north of the Broadway and Columbus intersection. Don't go looking for a beach. The neighbourhood is crammed with grocery stores, pastry shops, pizzerias and Neapolitan restaurants. It was here that the beat generation flourished in the late 1950s, inspired by the circle of poets and writers who spurned conventional society. Among them were Allen Ginsberg, Jack Kerouac and William Burroughs; they met at the poet Lawrence Ferlinghetti's City Lights Bookshop.

Financial District

Between Chinatown and the ferry landing stage cluster San Francisco's skyscrapers, among them the celebrated Transamerica Pyramid (600 Montgomery Street), one of the most outstanding features of the San Franciscan skyline. The business district is full of life at midday, when office workers go down into the streets for their lunch break, but deserted outside office hours. Several museums have a business theme: the Wells & Fargo Bank History Museum (420 Montgomery) traces the history of stagecoaches and early means of transporting money; the Pacific Heritage Museum (608 Commercial) is devoted to the region's economic activities and to currency.

Market Street

The main thoroughfare of the city centre, Market Street begins ultra-chic where it brushes the Financial District, becoming less distinguished as it heads south-

SAN FRANCISCO

west in the direction of the Civic Center (and even less so beyond). Boutiques and department stores give way to administrative buildings: the baroque City Hall, a massive Library and the Performing Arts Center, in whose Opera House the United Nations Charter was signed in 1945.

SoMa
South of the avenue stretches a district whose name is simply a contraction of South of Market (SoMa). Once a rather disreputable area, it has been rehabilitated and now figures among San Francisco's trendiest haunts. It centres on the Yerba Buena Gardens and the Museum of Modern Art (SFMOMA), in a modern building designed by Swiss architect Mario Botta. The beautifully illuminated upper galleries display masterpieces by Matisse, Manet, Monet, Picasso, Klee, Miró and Dali, among others.

The nearby Cartoon Art Museum (655 Mission St) features the strip cartoon.

Japantown
Pagodas and temples cluster round the Cultural and Trade Centre of Japantown, where you can take a course in Ikebana

Mario Botta chose zebra stripes for the turret of the Museum of Modern Art.

flower arrangement, learn how to make sushis, or stay in a typically Japanese hotel with sunken bathtubs, tatamis, kimonoed maids and indoor rock gardens. Access to the district is through a traditional torii gateway. Why not take part in a traditional tea ceremony? There's a Japanese tea room at Nichi Bei Kai, 1759 Sutter Street, run by the Japanese American Tea Society.

Haight-Ashbury

This gracious old residential district, which still preserves the lovely homes spared by the 1906 catastrophe, is famous for being the birthplace in the 1960s of the hippy movement. It lies west of the Civic Center, out towards Golden Gate Park. The pacifist ideal may have lost much of its fervour, but you can still enjoy the same spectacular view over the city centre: from Alamo Park, the skyscrapers form a magnificent backdrop to the Victorian houses on Steiner Street.

To the south, Castro is a favourite hangout of the gay community, which in the late 1970s established itself as the country's largest.

Golden Gate Park

Closed to traffic on Sundays, this park is a giant recreational area in the centre of town, and home to a number of museums. The splendid Asian Art Museum boasts more than 10,000 exhibits; paintings, sculpture, ceramics, jades, textiles, shown on a rotational basis. The California Academy of Sciences has an excellent museum of natural history, an aquarium and a planetarium. The M.H. de Young Memorial Museum features American arts from colonial times to the present day. The Strybing Arboretum displays collections of plants from California, Australia and the Mediterranean. There is also a Japanese Tea Garden and several lakes.

All kinds of organized activities take place in the park. On weekends, San Franciscans come here to cycle or roller skate (if

---

LEVIS AND LINGUISTICS

In 1848, with the first wave of the Gold Rush, a Jewish trader from Bavaria called Levi Strauss arrived in San Francisco with a bale of canvas sheets. Unable to sell them, he hit on the idea of having them made up into trousers for the prospectors. Unusually tough and hardwearing, they were an immediate success. The word *denim* was derived because the fabric came from Nîmes, France ("de Nîmes"). The word jeans came from the name of the port from where it was exported—Genoa (Gênes).

you want to join in you can hire your wheels on the spot) or to fly kites. The park stretches down to Ocean Beach, where many wet-suited surfers brave the chilly waters, which rarely warm up to more than 10°C (50°F). Enjoy a pleasant dinner at Cliff House, 1090 Point Lobos Avenue, to the sound of waves breaking on the rocks.

The Palace of the Legion of Honor, in neighbouring Lincoln Park, encloses an art museum of unexpected beauty (paintings from the 14th to 19th centuries, Rodin sculptures, furniture, etc.).

Mission

South of Castro and southeast of Golden Gate, Mission is the veritable birthplace of San Francisco. The Spanish founded their first mission here in 1776 and called it Dolorès. Dedicated to St Francis of Assisi, it was one of 21 such establishments scattered along the Camino Real, each one a day's walk from the next. It also bestowed on San Francisco its name. Some of the scenes in Alfred Hitchcock's *Vertigo* were filmed here. The local community is predominantly Hispanic, and the surrounding area is well known for its murals.

The Islands

Of the various excursions which are available in San Francisco Bay, the most tempting is probably the trip to the old island-prison of Alcatraz. The name comes from the Spanish *alcatraces*, or "pelicans".

Alcatraz

Known as The Rock, this dry and desolate island, 500 m (550 yd) long can be clearly seen from Fisherman's Wharf. It was used as a high-security prison between 1934 and 1963, and it's claimed that no prisoner ever escaped from Alcatraz, not even its most celebrated inmate Al Capone, who spent four years behind its bars. In fact, 36 desperate prisoners did make an attempt at escaping, and five of those have never been accounted for. In principle, the strong currents, cold waters and hungry sharks would have made it impossible to survive the 2,400-m (2,600-yd) swim, and it's believed they must have drowned. Nevertheless, one man did make it to the shore in 1962, only to be recaptured and reimprisoned.

This extraordinarily high security had its price, and the penitentiary was closed in 1963 because of the exorbitant expense needed to run it—each inmate costing the American taxpayers the not inconsiderable sum of $40,000 per year. Every prisoner had a daily hot shower in imported fresh water, which in theory was designed to prevent them from becoming acclimatized to the low temperature of the sea.

The cells and facilities are all rather sinister and extremely dilapidated. With grim humour, the prisoners named the rows of cells after celebrated American thoroughfares such as Park Avenue and Sunset Boulevard.

Treasure Island

This island is worth a visit if only for the spectacular view it provides of San Francisco. It serves as a stepping stone for the Oakland Bay Bridge which crosses the narrows on the eastern side, and is ideally situated directly opposite the city. Close to the naval base is a viewpoint, from where the scene is particularly impressive at dusk when the skyline gradually lights up against a glowing orange background.

The Bay Area

There are several places worth visiting within a radius of 50 km (30 miles) around the bay, mostly to the north: the resort of Sausalito, the University of Berkeley, the Napa and Sonoma valleys where California's most prestigious vineyards are found, Muir Woods and Point Reyes Park.

GREEN POWER

East of San Francisco, all along Route 580, thousands of wind turbines have sprouted on the flowered hillsides. A symbol of the 1990s enthusiasm for alternative energy sources, these windmills supply electricity to the towns in the vicinity of Tracy, but function only at 25 per cent of their capacity. The drawbacks: they require a great deal of land; they are noisy; the wind does not blow at peak speeds all the time; and even worse, thousands of birds, including hawk, owl and golden eagle have been killed by the blades.

SAN FRANCISCO

Sausalito
Immediately to the north of the Golden Gate Bridge there are two charming small ports of Mediterranean appearance: Sausalito, with the air of a holiday resort, and Tiburon, more residential. Each spreads over the top of a hill, with sumptuous villas scattered across the slopes. Many artists and intellectuals have felt the irresistible pull and settled here. Sausalito started life as a Portuguese fishing village, but since the establishment of the San Francisco Yacht Club, it has grown into a large marina and tourist centre, with shops and cafés lining the quayside and a floating village of houseboats. There's a regular ferry service between the two ports and San Francisco.

Berkeley
On the east coast of the Bay, near the town of Oakland, is the campus of Berkeley University. The easiest way to get there is to take the BART (Bay Area Rapid Transit), the underground railway crossing the Bay—and the San Andreas Fault. The Visitor Centre is located in the main lobby of the Student Union Building; you can wander around the campus on your own or follow one of the 1½-hour guided tours led by students, who will show you a classroom, the library, the sports facilities, and so on.

One of the great seats of learning of the west coast, the university has had as many as 20 Nobel Prize winners on the staff at the same time, but despite such eminence it did not escape the student revolts of the 1960s.

Known for its theatre and museums (of art, anthropology and palaeontology), the small town around the campus is a pleasant place to visit. Telegraph Street, leading to the university, bustles with trendy student life. Near Shattuck Avenue, restaurants take over, earning the district the title of Gourmet Ghetto.

1

THE MOST VENERABLE TREE Not long ago, you could drive a car through the tunnelled-out trunk of the Tunnel Log in Sequoia National Park. After it toppled, the mantle of fame passed to **General Sherman**, the oldest-known sequoia at the grand old age of 5,000 years, standing 83 m (272 ft) high. It takes 20 people to link arms all round the trunk, which measures 30 m (98 ft) in circumference at the base.

Wine Country

Leaving San Francisco by the Golden Gate and travelling east for an hour on Route 116, you will come upon the first serried ranks of vines. Napa and Sonoma, two parallel valleys, produce most of the best Californian vintages. There are around 200 wineries in the Napa County and around 150 in Sonoma County, occupying some 25,000 hectares (62,000 acres) of land.

The first vines were imported from Europe, mainly France and Italy, in 1857. Though the labels on the bottles bear a resemblance to French vintages, don't mistake the Californian wines for pale imitations of their Gallic counterparts. Each wine produced here has its own personality, being in general headier because of the greater exposure to the sun. It was these very vines which largely contributed to the replanting of French vineyards after the disastrous invasion of phylloxera in the 1870s. Moreover, renowned French names such as Mumm, Taittinger and Moët et Chandon now produce in this area.

Most of the vineyards offer guided tours with tasting of the product included (they often charge a small fee). The most prestigious wines are the red Cabernet Sauvignon, Pinot Noir and Zinfandel, and the white Chardonnay.

In the historic town of Sonoma, visit the San Francisco Solano Mission, founded in 1823, the northernmost on the Camino Real. The plaza is surrounded by stone buildings and adobe houses from the Mexican era.

Muir Woods

Situated 25 km (16 miles) north of San Francisco on the slopes of Mt Tamalpais, the Muir Woods nature reserve encompasses a sumptuous forest of giant redwoods (sequoias) nearly a thousand years old. The uppermost branches of the tallest trees reach to more than 70 m (230 ft). The William Kent Memorial Tree is the tallest at 83 m (270 ft).

Point Reyes

Continuing north along the rim of the Pacific Ocean, the road winds past attractive white frame farmhouses which the San Franciscans have adopted as their country residences. It leads to Point Reyes peninsula, separated from the mainland by the San Andreas Fault. This coastal reserve is a haven for migratory birds, many of which can be observed at Drake's Bay. Sir Francis Drake landed here in 1579 and took possession of California in the name of Queen Elizabeth I of England. The broad green hills of the southern side of the park descend to a wide sandy beach.

THE CENTRAL COAST
Monterey, Carmel, Big Sur, Hearst Castle, Santa Barbara

From San Francisco to San Luis Obispo, Highway 1 hugs the contours of the Coastal Range barrier. Battered by storms and waves, this rocky coast—clad with stunted pines on the northern side—is a refuge for a large number of animal species.

Monterey

At the south end of the bay of the same name, Monterey—two hours by car from San Francisco—is an old fishing port which has now become a holiday resort. The town was built round a mission founded in 1770 by Junípero Serra, and was the capital of upper California under the Spanish and then the Mexicans. Little of its past is still visible apart from the adobe church on Church Street, now called the Royal Presidio Chapel.

At Fisherman's Wharf, the quayside is lined with shops and restaurants. You can visit the Stevenson House at 530 Houston Street, where the writer Robert Louis Stevenson spent several months after his arrival from Scotland. Local tradition has it that he found inspiration for some of his scenes in *Treasure Island* in the craggy coast of the region. More recently, Monterey has been the setting for many of Steinbeck's novels.

Monterey Bay Aquarium

Cannery Row, abandoned in the 1940s, has been converted in part to shops and is now the home of one of the best aquariums in the world. It has several pools which contain a vast array of species common to the cold waters of the Californian coast, including sea otters, octopuses, jellyfish and sharks. A huge tank recreates an underwater kelp forest, in which the seaweed can grow to lengths of 100 m (330 ft).

Carmel

From Monterey to Carmel, a minor toll road known as the 17 Mile Drive clings to every curve of the shoreline. It takes you through Pacific Grove, a pleasant town of Victorian villas, before following the rim of the Pacific Ocean. The view of the sea is as exhilarating as the cool wind that permanently refreshes this coast Seal Rocks and Bird Rocks are home to colonies of seals, pelicans and sea lions.

Anacapa, one of the eight untamed Channel Islands.

THE CENTRAL COAST

After passing the numerous golf courses of Pebble Beach, the road brings you to Carmel. This most attractive and refined of towns was the home of numerous artists and writers at the beginning of the 20th century. The narrow shady streets are crammed with art galleries and restaurants. The San Carlos Borromeo Mission was established here in 1770. Its founder, Junípero Serra, lived here until his death in 1784 and is buried in the cemetery behind the church.

CAMINO REAL

In 1767 the Spanish in Mexico launched into plans to set up missions in California. The Franciscan monk Junípero Serra was given the responsibility for organizing the project. The first wooden mission building was constructed in 1769 at San Diego, just north of the Mexican frontier. The following year, the mission at Monterey was built, and before the death of Serra in 1784 nine other churches were erected. In all, 21 missions were to be founded on part of the old Camino Real, on the stretch between San Diego and San Francisco. The royal road itself covered almost 3,000 km (1,800 miles) from Mexico City to Santa Fe.

Point Lobos

A few miles south of Carmel, the Point Lobos State Reserve, its cliffs falling steeply down to the ocean, shelters a host of animal species. Sea otters stake their claim here and can be observed at China Cove or Gibson Beach, floating on their back on a mattress of kelp. At Sea Lion Cove, the bathing belles on the beach are seals rather than sea lions, and between January and April you may be able to spot migrating whales further out, on their way between Alaska and Mexico.

Big Sur

South of Carmel, the highway twists alarmingly along the steep coastal strip. The Big Sur region with its many nature reserves is a favourite destination of town-dwellers who dream of camping, fishing or rambling in unspoilt countryside. A couple of solitary houses with wide bay windows gaze towards the sea. The relaxed atmosphere has attracted many artists and writers: Henry Miller spent several years here.

At Big Sur itself, there is a large forest of giant redwoods in the Pfeiffer Big Sur Park. This is not to be confused with the Julia Pfeiffer Burns State Park further south, where a walk of a few minutes along a pretty path leads to a view of a waterfall plunging directly into the sea.

The landscapes of the Big Sur region provide inspiration for artists and writers.

Hearst Castle

The gigantic home of press magnate William Randolph Hearst, now converted to a museum, is perched high in the hills at San Simeon. The inspiration for the Orson Welles film *Citizen Kane*, Hearst became a passionate collector of works of art after a voyage to Europe. He spent countless sums decorating the 146 rooms of his "castle", which was still under construction at his death in 1951, fully 32 years after building first began.

All styles are represented in an unbelievable mish-mash of Greek and Roman, Gothic and baroque, genuine and fake alike. A 32-m (105-ft) swimming pool lined with Roman mosaics and surrounded by colonnades lies at the foot of a copy of Donatello's statue of *David*. The bedroom contains the bed of Cardinal Richelieu, minister of the French king Louis XIII. In the corridors you will come across everything from statues of Egyptian gods to Roman sarcophagi. The main dining room, where a succession of the rich and famous—Greta Garbo, Charlie Chaplin, Winston Churchill and more—were entertained, is decorated with church choir stalls and a cedarwood ceiling from an Italian monastery. To see this eclectic wonderland, you

have to take one of the guided tours leaving from the Visitor Center. A bus transports you the 8 km (5 miles) to the castle through what was once Hearst's private zoo. Departures are at fixed times and the tour takes a minimum of 90 minutes. But be warned, this is the most visited attraction in California after Disneyland, and you should reserve your tour on tel. 1-800-444-4445.

Santa Barbara

Beside the intensely blue Pacific Ocean, the prosperous town proclaims its Hispanic roots. The brick-paved, palm-lined streets, a few old buildings and modern ones built in the same Spanish style, make this a charming spot. The main street, State Street, where art galleries and small quiet cafés are legion, is the place to go for shopping and strolling. The pedestrian zone of Paseo is ideal for lunch at a restaurant terrace. The Santa Barbara Museum of Art (1130 State Street) is considered one of the best galleries of regional art in the country.

North of the town, Mission Santa Barbara, "Queen of the Missions", founded in 1786, is the largest Franciscan monastery in California. The restored church and outbuildings can be visited on a self-guided tour.

To get a better overview of the town's Spanish past, drop in at the History Museum, set in a beautiful building dating from 1819, or the historical museum in the Presidio, a fortress erected in 1782 to guard the Camino Real.

Despite its historical background, Santa Barbara is nevertheless definitely part of modern-day Southern California. Along the pleasant seafront, several miles long, joggers, cyclists and rollerbladers exercise under the coconut palms. You can hire a bicycle or even a tricycle if you're a bit shaky on two wheels, watch

---

LOMPOC VALLEY

The town of Lompoc west of Santa Barbara is California's main flower-growing centre. The development of innovative blooms is a major activity, and 20 per cent of world's annual production of a hundred or so new floral hybrids come from here. Known as the "Valley of Flowers", Lompoc Valley is an extraordinary place where flower growers cultivate more than 500 varieties on some 5,000 acres. In summer, the huge fields of poppies, marigolds and sweet peas make a brilliant patchwork of colours.

Santa Barbara has a decidedly Hispanic air.

the volley ball games, visit the Maritime Museum or stroll along the magnificent beach.

Solvang

Some 40 km (25 miles) northwest of Santa Barbara by Route 101, Solvang is definitely the most original of all California's small towns. Settled by Danes as of 1911, it has developed into a very lively Scandinavian cultural centre. All the buildings have been integrated to reproduce an authentic Danish village with typical windmills, bakeries and clogmakers' shops, not to mention the pubs serving draught Carlsberg. Don't be surprised if you hear Scandinavian languages spoken in the street—the community's Nordic traditions are passed on from one generation to the next and remain very much alive.

Channel Islands

The eight unspoilt islands off the southern coast, five of which are part of a national park, form one of the richest animal sanctuaries in California. Sea lions and sea elephants, seals and other species frequent the rocky coasts of Santa Barbara Island, San Miguel,

---

THE EARTH MOVES

The infamous San Andreas Fault passes through California in the region of San Francisco, marking the boundary between the American and Pacific tectonic plates. There were irregular but sizeable earthquakes all over the area throughout the 20th century. In 1906, a terrible convulsion estimated at 8.25 on the Richter Scale destroyed 80 per cent of San Francisco, causing more than 500 deaths. Even more serious was the huge fire which followed, impossible to control because of damage to the water conduits. Santa Barbara endured its own earthquake in 1925. San Francisco was rapidly rebuilt and suffered no further major quakes until quite recently. During the summer of 1989, a shock of magnitude 7 caused the partial destruction of the bridge between San Francisco and Oakland across the Bay. However, the stringent anti-earthquake building regulations in force proved their effectiveness and the number of victims on this occasion was very few. Most recently, in January 1994, Los Angeles felt a tremor comparable in magnitude to that of 1989. But Californians, proud of their state, are quick to tell you that they would rather risk an earthquake here than live in safety anywhere else.

Anacapa and, to a lesser extent, Santa Rosa. During the migratory season—mainly from January to April—schools of grey whales arriving from Alaska meet others making the return journey, slapping the surface of the open sea with their forked tails and spouting columns of water in the air.

A trip from Ventura or Santa Barbara with one of the many tour operators will enable you to disembark on most of the islands. If you want to stay on any island other than Santa Catalina for a few days, then you must be prepared to camp.

Santa Catalina, at the southern end, is the most developed of the Channel Islands. It is easily accessible by ferry or catamaran from San Pedro, Long Beach, Newport Beach or Dana Point. The only town on the island is Avalon, tucked around a small bay beneath craggy mountains. It boasts an astonishing Art Deco casino built in 1929 which can be visited with a guided tour. Santa Catalina is excellent for diving and watersports in general. No cars are allowed, so you must visit the interior on foot or take the organized tour.

MONARCHS

Several forests along the Californian coast play host to quite exceptional gatherings. Monarch butterflies, whose lifespan is rather longer than that of most other lepidoptera, migrate southwards from the rest of the US and Canada to spend the winter in warmer climes. Most head for Mexico, but some stop off on the way. From October to February, the eucalyptus in the Julia Pfeiffer Burns State Park and Pismo State Park are covered in tens of thousands of these butterflies, massed in clusters on the branches.

THE TWO MOST BEAUTIFUL MISSIONS Along the California coast, a few vestiges of the Spanish past provide a pleasant pretext for breaking your journey. The **"Queen of the Missions"** at Santa Barbara is the biggest Franciscan mission in the entire state. North on the Camino Real, the **Carmel Mission**, which has become a basilica, is the most picturesque in northern California.

SIERRA NEVADA
Yosemite, Mammoth Lakes, Lake Mono, Sequoia and Kings Canyon

At the same latitude as San Francisco and a few hours away by road, the Sierra Nevada harbours some of California's preferred destinations.

Yosemite

The park covers 3,000 sq km (1,160 sq miles) of some of the most beautiful country of the Sierra Nevada. It is one of the best sites in the United States to study flora and fauna. Wolves and bears inhabit the more remote areas, and deer, beavers, marmots and ground squirrels abound.

Yosemite Valley itself is characterized by rocky walls. The most famous, El Capitan, offers 900 m (nearly 3,000 ft) of sheer challenge to rock climbers. A typical glaciated valley, it is encircled by peaks reaching up to 4,000 m (13,000 ft). Made famous by the naturalist John Muir and photographer Ansel Adams, Yosemite Valley is the spectacular heart of the National Park. Most of the hiking trails leave from here. One of the most popular leads to the Vernal Falls and the Nevada Fall, at their best just after the snows melt in spring. Allow three hours to walk up and two hours to come back down.

On the north side of the valley, another path leads first to the bottom of Yosemite Falls and then on up to the top. These falls plummet down more than 700 m (2,300 ft) in three stages. If you don't want to make the climb, admire the view from the rocky promontory of Glacier Point, accessible by road. The entire valley of Yosemite and that of Merced spread out before you.

Mammoth Lakes

A short distance from Yosemite over the Tioga Pass (closed from October to May), the elegant Mammoth Lakes is one of California's leading winter-sports resorts. The ski runs are ideal for beginners and expert skiers alike. All the facilities you would expect from a large resort are available.

To make a change from skiing, you can hire a snowmobile to take you around, possibly covering the 16 km (10 miles) or so to Devil's Postpile, an impressive group of basalt columns resembling organ pipes. These are the vestiges of an ancient lava flow. Only the park bus is allowed to

Yosemite Valley dressed in its autumn finery.

use the minor road leading to this natural "monument", at an altitude of 2,500 m (8,200 ft), open from July to October.

Lake Mono

At the foot of the eastern slopes of the Sierra Nevada, the intense blue waters of Lake Mono reflect the eternal snows above. The water has produced bizarre concretions: towers of limestone tufa (calcium carbonate) resulting from the chemical reaction between the salt water of the lake and the springs of fresh water which bubble up through its bed. Some of these structures are estimated to be almost 13,000 years old. The most easily accessible are situated on the south bank along Route 120, 8 km (5 miles) from the junction with Route 395.

These formations are normally under the surface, and if we can see them today, it is thanks to the city of Los Angeles: Lake Mono is the principal source of water for the city, and since 1948 its level dropped by more than 12 m (40 ft). In the process, the salt content doubled.

Bodie

Very close to Lake Mono, Bodie, built during the Gold Rush, can be considered the most beautiful ghost town of the American West. At one time its inhabitants numbered several thousand. The bank and prison, the remains of the Chinese quarter, together with a few scattered houses, still stand, forlorn memories of the Wild West. The town is accessible only in summer, as the road is blocked by snow each winter.

Sequoia and Kings Canyon

Sequoia National Park was founded in 1890 to protect the redwoods from over-exploitation. These giant trees, which first appeared at the beginning of the tertiary era, can grow to more than 80 m (260 ft) and live for more than 4,000 years. Their bark, which grows up to 60 cm (2 ft) thick, protects them from insects and fire.

The park has 32 groups of sequoias, reached by paths. One of the most popular is the 3-km (2-mile) Congress Trail. Look out for the 2,500-year-old General Sherman Tree, at 83 m (272 ft) the tallest tree on earth. Its circumference at ground level is 32 m (105 ft).

In Kings Canyon, you can see the General Grant Tree. This area of the park is ideal for hiking and boasts some magnificent walls of granite.

Tufa towers make a handy perch for migratory birds: more than 300 species flock to Lake Mono.

LOS ANGELES
City of Angels, Hollywood, West L.A., Anaheim

City of Angels

In the 19th century, Nuestra Señora la Reina de los Angeles was a simple village built around a mission. With the Gold Rush and the coming of the national railroad to California, floods of immigrants began to colonize the desert to the south. The town developed rapidly, expanding from 1,500 in 1850 to 300,000 in 1908, when the cinema studios opened. The discovery of oil brought thousands more hopefuls. The San Fernando Valley to the north became a market gardening centre for all the West Coast. The production of oranges was a success from the beginning, foreshadowing the formidable harvests of modern times. From its agricultural beginnings, Los Angeles grew to become an industrial metropolis with World War II.

After barely a century of expansion, Los Angeles has now become a veritable megalopolis with over 10 million inhabitants. And people still continue to arrive, 300,000 of them every year: immigrants from exotic lands, and bright-eyed domestic migrants from the chillier, drabber parts of the country, seeking their fortune under the warming sun. Never mind the problems of smog, noise, racial tension and traffic overload—there's a balmy city at the end of the rainbow, where anyone can find a crock of gold.

Los Angeles is not a city, but a state of mind. It has no traditional sense of a downtown urban core interacting with surrounding neighbourhoods. Instead, it's a motley patchwork of scores of separate and very diverse communities, all stitched together by the nation's most heavily travelled motorways. But you can't deter the dreamers, and if they can't find enough escapism in L.A., they can pursue their fantasies out of town: at Beverly Hills, Sunset Boulevard, Santa Monica and Hollywood, or at the original Disneyland, still one of the world's most popular tourist attractions.

Downtown

It may not have a heart but it does have a core, centred on the buildings of the financial quarter and its one and only thoroughfare, Olivera Street. Here you will see many restaurants and the last vestiges of the Mexican pueblo. You

The stunning Walt Disney Concert Hall, designed by Frank Gehry, illuminates downtown L.A.

will also find Avila Adobe, the oldest house in Los Angeles, dating from 1818.

It's worth looking closely at the architecture of this area, as you tread the recently renovated streets of the centre, lined with administrative and cultural buildings. You will note the number of murals: L.A. is called the mural capital of the United States, and you can join a bus tour to see some of the most striking works.

A large group of buildings makes up the Music Center. Next door, the Museum of Contemporary Art (MOCA, 250 South Grand Avenue) houses a permanent collection of post-1940 paintings by major artists such as Rothko and Kline. At 136 W 4th St (between Main and Spring), the Museum of Neon Art is the only one of its kind in the world devoted to this most American of disciplines.

From the top of City Hall you can enjoy an uninterrupted view of the city. On the corner of Grand and First streets, the matt-finished stainless-steel Walt Disney Concert Hall, designed by Frank Gehry on the curving lines of his Guggenheim Museum in Bilbao, is the dazzling new home of the Los Angeles Philharmonic. The 2,265-seat hall was partly funded by Disney's widow Lillian, on the condition that there had to be a public garden. It took 16 years to complete (and in the meantime the estimated cost more than doubled). The highlight of the gardens is a rose-shaped fountain made from pieces of Delft china.

To the southeast, near 1st and Central Streets, is Little Tokyo and its Japanese Village Mall, a shopping centre in Japanese style. Chinatown, north of the Civic Center, has many restaurants and shops, notably along its pedestrian street, Gin Ling Way.

Exposition Park to the south, at the junction of Figueroa Street and Exposition Boulevard, was one of the venues of the 1984 Olympic Games. It also encompasses four museums: the California Science Center (IMAX cinema), the Natural History Museum, the Aerospace Museum of California and the California African American Museum (CAAM), tracing the history of the black community in the Golden State.

Pasadena

Northeast of the city centre, Pasadena, one of the original districts of Los Angeles, has several fine museums. At 234 Museum Drive, the Southwest Museum of the American Indian is currently closed for renovation and will be moving to a new, more spacious home in 2009, but its Museum Store remains open at weekends.

More than 6 million rare editions cram the shelves of the Huntington Library at San Marino, 1151 Oxford Road, surrounded by luxuriant gardens.

The outstanding Norton Simon Museum, 411 West Colorado Boulevard, focuses mainly on Impressionist painting, but you will also find collections of drawings, sculptures, etc.

Hollywood

The big white letters on the hillside have been spelling out its name since the 1920s. When Charlie Chaplin turned up here in 1913, there was little more than the horse barn where Cecil B. DeMille had just finished shooting his first film. During the following decade, all the great producers headed for Southern California, drawn by the perfect climate and the wonderful landscapes.

The Studios

The barn has been moved to Highland Boulevard, where it serves as the Hollywood Heritage Museum, dedicated to the silent screen (visits by appointment only). Most of the other studios have gravitated north to Burbank or the San Fernando Valley, except for Paramount which has stayed at 5555 Melrose Avenue.

Universal Studios Hollywood on Lankershim Boulevard, just north of the Hollywood Freeway, is a major attraction for those who want to see behind the scenes. The guides have all the showbiz flair of Hollywood itself, but the tour of the film sets is only half the fun. There are also amusement park rides and attractions based on memorable adventure movies, from *Jurassic Park* to *Shrek*.

Hollywood Boulevard

After a period in the doldrums, the famous avenue is trying to rediscover some of its past splendour. Embedded in the pavement are more than 2,500 bronze stars engraved with the great names of showbiz. On Vine Street, Marlon Brando is near No. 2765; Marilyn Monroe in front of No. 6774; John Wayne at No. 1541.

The handprints of Hollywood idols are preserved for posterity in the cement courtyard of Mann's Chinese Theatre, 6925 Hollywood Boulevard. When Sid Graumann's great exotic cinema was inaugurated in 1927, actress Constance Talmadge tripped and fell onto the fresh cement. The incident became a tradition as Graumann persuaded all the stars who attended gala premieres at the movie house to get down on their knees and leave their mark. A few artists had more original ideas: Fred Astaire left his footprints, Marilyn Monroe her high

Los Angeles

Murals brighten up many a blank wall, all over the city.

heels, Betty Grable her legs, and Jimmy Durante his famous schnozzle.

Behind the theatre, two huge white elephants dominate the entrance of the Hollywood & Highland Center, a shopping mall with nightclubs and the Kodak Theatre, where the Oscars ceremony takes place.

At no. 7021, the Hollywood Entertainment Museum gives a behind-the-scenes view of film-making, while its shop sells film stars' clothing and costumes, as well as stage props from vintage and recent films.

At 1666 N Highland Avenue, the Art Deco Max Factor Building has been carefully restored to house the fascinating Hollywood History Museum.

Griffith Park

North of Hollywood sprawls Los Angeles' biggest park covering a vast piece of land bequeathed by a wealthy Welsh immigrant. At the weekend, city residents meet up in the park to stroll or ride bikes or horses.

Within the park, the Gene Autry Western Heritage Museum, named after a Western film actor, is devoted exclusively to the history of the conquest of the West. The immense Travel Town Transportation Museum displays steam locomotives, ancient fire engines and other highlights.

The nearby Griffith Observatory houses a state-of-the-art planetarium and hosts exhibitions devoted to astronomy—visits by reservation only. There's a splendid view over Los Angeles from here.

West L.A.

South of Hollywood Boulevard is the famous Sunset Boulevard. The Hollywood section is known simply as "the Strip". Sleazy nightclubs and cheap motels stand side by side with hip boutiques and elegant restaurants.

Further west, Sunset Boulevard becomes more sinuous and residential. West Hollywood, crammed with art galleries, shops and restaurants, is now one of the most fashionable places to live. An assortment of shops line lively Melrose Avenue. On the south side, Farmer's Market (at Fairfax and Third), founded in the 1930s Depression, is an immense outdoor food market.

Museums

There are several museums on Wilshire Boulevard. The George C. Page Museum (5801 Wilshire) displays some of the many animal fossils, including those of tigers, bears, bison and wolves, discovered in a nearby tar deposit.

The Los Angeles County Museum of Art (5905 Wilshire) has collections of paintings and oriental art, together with a sculpture garden.

Beverly Hills

The sumptuous villas and splendid gardens of the rich and famous follow one after the other in a dazzling riot of styles: Bauhaus, Gothic, Spanish, English, and so on. Drive through this suburb of quiet little streets. Carolwood Drive was home to Barbara Streisand (No. 325), Walt Disney (No. 355) and Gregory Peck (No. 375). Elvis Presley spent several years at 144 Monovale Drive, where it intersects with Sunset Boulevard. Summit Drive was home to Charlie Chaplin (No. 1085) and silent movie stars Mary Pickford and Douglas Fairbanks.

Once a bare hillside pitted with oil wells, the area began to develop when the Beverly Hills Hotel, the watering-hole of the movie stars, was built. Elegant Rodeo Drive reeks of luxury; it is full of the world's most exclusive shops for leather goods, jewellery and designer clothes.

At 9786 W Pico Boulevard, the Museum of Tolerance deals with the history of racial conflict in the United States—with a whole section dedicated to the Holocaust.

Further west is the stylish district of Bel Air, south of which is Westwood, seat of the University of California (UCLA). The campus contains several museums: art, ethnography, sculpture. In addition, you can view Armand Hammer's superb collection of European masterpieces at 10899 Wilshire Boulevard.

Santa Monica

The terminus of Route 66, which in the 1930s saw a steady stream of incomers from Kansas and Oklahoma, Santa Monica opens onto a wide beach kissed by the Pacific waves. At weekends, residents descend on this western extension of the city to bask in the sun or play sports. On the track running alongside the ribbon of sand, at the foot of the palm trees of Palisades Park, roller skaters and cyclists come to practise or to demonstrate their skills.

Getty Center

The splendid Getty Center, in the Santa Monica Mountains above the San Diego Freeway, consists of six buildings designed by Richard Meier. It features the new J. Paul Getty Museum and several art-oriented institutes. The collections, some of the finest in the United States, include illuminated manuscripts, sculpture, photographs, drawings, pre-20th-century European painting and the decorative arts. The canvases are displayed on the first floor under skylights. The hour-long tour is a good way to see the highlights of the collections.

Malibu

The most westerly of the Los Angeles communities, with a beach that's popular with surfers, Malibu is the bastion of movie stars and other exceedingly prosperous citizens.

The Getty Villa, the billionaire's former ranch house-turned-museum, modelled on the Papyrus Villa at Herculaneum (near Pompeii), displays Etruscan, Greek and Roman antiquities. More than 1,200 pieces from the extensive collection of approximately 44,000 works of art are on view. Entry is free, but you need to book in advance.

Anaheim

Anaheim is 40 km (25 miles) south of Los Angeles and boasts several sights in addition to the world-famous Disneyland Resort.

Disneyland Resort

This is the leading attraction in the whole of California. From the moment you enter, you are plunged into a world of make-believe. The complex is split into two separate theme parks: Disney's California Adventure Park and Disneyland Park, with more restaurants, shops and entertainment grouped in Downtown Disney, and four large hotels.

The original Disneyland Park is divided into eight "lands". Shop-lined Main Street sets the tone with its sunny evocation of small-town USA at the turn of the century. You may notice that the buildings are all three-quarter size: in this effort to escape from harsh reality, everything is a little smaller than life.

Adventureland is a boat ride through simulated jungle foliage on a river that flows through Asia, Africa and South America. Tigers and elephants cavort amongst the foliage, against a background of jungle noises.

A miniature train hurtles through Frontierland, the pioneer country of the Old West. You barely have time to turn around before you are whisked away on a paddleboat cruise around Davy Crockett Island.

The entrance to Fantasyland, the fairytale kingdom, is through Sleeping Beauty's pink castle.

One of the most exciting themes is Tomorrowland, constantly being renovated to keep pace with technological progress. You can take a trip to Mars aboard the Star Tours spaceship, or experience the thrills of Space Mountain, a rollercoaster ride in the dark through a starry sky.

New Orleans Square is the Disney version of the old city's French Quarter, featuring strolling jazz musicians, Caribbean pirates and a haunted house.

Mickey's Toontown is a 3-D gathering of the mouse and his friends, while Critter Country is inhabited by the lovable bear Winnie the Pooh, Tigger, Eeyore and other favourites.

Disney's California Adventure Park presents over 30 new attractions spread over four "lands", with many exclusive rides. Among them is the delightful Jumpin' Jellyfish, where you float up and down gently beneath a parachute as if you were underwater.

Knott's Berry Farm

To the south, Knott's Berry Farm recreates the atmosphere of the Old West. Picture a ghost town duly assembled piece by piece from abandoned desert towns, with saloon, train station, prison, gun store—and of course a brothel. You can visit a mine, be attacked on a train or try your hand at gold prospecting.

Long Beach

The majestic liner *Queen Mary*, now a floating hotel and maritime museum, lies permanently at anchor here. You can also visit the Aquarium of the Pacific, one of the biggest in the world.

SAN DIEGO AND THE DESERT
San Diego, California Desert

The town of San Diego presides over the southern part of the Golden State, but the great Mojave Desert eclipses everything. Far from being a dull, empty wasteland, the desert region has plenty to see in its several first-class nature reserves.

San Diego
At the threshold of Mexico, San Diego saw the birth of California. It was the first harbour to be discovered (1542) on Spain's quest northwards from Mexico, and also the first site chosen for the establishment of a mission two centuries later. Today, San Diego is the second-largest city in the state after Los Angeles and one of the largest ports in North America. Thanks to its warm, dry climate and its superlative position on two sheltered bays, perhaps also because of its free-flowing traffic, it has been voted the most family-friendly city in the whole country.

The Centre
In the midst of the downtown skyscrapers, several blocks of restored Victorian houses make up the lively Gaslamp Quarter, full of little shops and cafés. Here you'll find a few minor museums, but the majority are grouped in Balboa Park to the northeast. They are devoted to natural history, sport, automobiles, aeronautics, science, photography, model trains, among others. The most interesting include the Museum of Art (1450 El Prado) and the Museum of Man (1350 El Prado), one of the finest anthropological exhibitions in the country. The park is also famous for its zoo, where the animals thrive in their natural settings.

The Old Town
West of Cabrillo Freeway and a few miles from the centre, the first constructions of the Old Town date from 1769, when the San Diego Mission at Alcala (further east, north of the Alvarado Freeway) was built. This old quarter is centred around Plaza Vieja, known as Plaza de Toros in Spanish times. Among the many restored adobe houses, numerous restaurants and shops strive to create a Mexican atmosphere.

The Bay
Opposite North Island, the Seaport Village complex of shops

Balboa Park is the site of many museums, and the zoo.

and restaurants overlooks the busy port. Close by, several 19th-century ships lie at anchor in front of the Maritime Museum. South of here, you can board an excursion boat at the Harbour Drive promenade to take a trip round the harbour.

For an uninterrupted view of the bay, visit Cabrillo National Monument on the Point Loma Promontory. From mid-December to March you may spot migrating whales passing by out in the deep waters.

> **CALIFORNIA DREAMING**
>
> When explorer Juan Rodríguez Cabrillo, in the service of the Viceroy of Mexico, landed near San Diego in 1542, he immediately came to the conclusion that this must be the "island of California", arbitrarily placed on the map a few years earlier by a Jesuit cartographer. Described in a novel by García Ordóñez de Montalvo, published in 1521, California was the name given to a mythical island situated "on the right hand of the Indian Empire… very close to earthly Paradise" and ruled by Queen Califia. The Jesuit, inspired by the recent discoveries in the New World, had simply given free rein to his imagination.

The SeaWorld adventure park on Mission Bay north of the town has a huge aquarium, and there are several shows and attractions feeaturing orcas (killer whales), dolphins, sea lions, polar bears and penguins.

Beaches and Surroundings

The sands of Silver Strand Beach, a coastal cordon encircling San Diego Bay, stretch for 40 km (25 miles) down to the Mexican border.

Close to the city, south of North Island, Coronado is a desirable residential area doubling with a pleasant seaside resort.

Northwards beyond Mission Bay, the sandy shore continues as far as La Jolla, where there is another branch of the Museum of Contemporary Art (MCA) at 700 Prospect Street (paintings and sculpture from 1950 to the present day). The Wild Animal Park at Escondido (15500 San Pasqual Valley Road) is a vast zoo where animals such as giraffe, okapi and elephant roam in a re-creation of their natural habitats.

California Desert

As you journey inland from the coast of Southern California, the built-up zones soon give way to the empty wastes of the Mojave Desert. This gigantic wilderness stretches all the way to Nevada, continuing further east and south

CALIFORNIA DESERT

The play of light and shadow in the sands of Death Valley.

as the Sonora Desert. It is one of the last intact arid ecosystems of the United States.

Anza Borrego

A good hour by road to the east of San Diego, Anza Borrego is the largest nature reserve in California. Its barren mountains and desert plains harbour a few rare oases; the biggest patch of green is Borrego Spring, where the park's visitor information centre is located.

From April until June the park is dazzling. For a few short weeks dozens of varieties of cactus and succulents flower in a riot of colour—pink, red, orange, yellow.

Palm Springs

One look at this resort cum retirement town in the middle of the Colorado Desert and it's clear that this is a retreat of the well-heeled—elegant, large homes with swimming pool and manicured lawn, over 80 golf courses in the vicinity, luxurious palace-like hotels, no garish sign or unsightly building to jar the general look of understated opulence.

It's hard to realise that not long ago Palm Springs was just a small town on the railway line with a couple of shops and some adobe houses. In the 1930s Hollywood discovered what a pleasant spot the little backwater town

was with its dry climate and healthy hot springs. The barren land was beautified with some 50,000 palm trees, gardens and swimming pools, made possible with the installation of irrigation networks.

A cable car will take you up from torrid desert to mountaintop pine forests, snow-encrusted in winter. The views are spectacular. Down below are several interesting museums to keep you busy when you tire of lazing by the pool. The Palm Springs Art Museum (101 Museum Drive) concentrates on modern artworks and also includes collections of Indian and mesoamerican artworks. The Living Desert museum is a superb zoo and botanical garden displaying desert flora.

Joshua Tree

Half-way between Los Angeles and the Arizona border, the park is the home of the unique Joshua Tree. Growing only at altitudes between 800 and 1,300 m (2,600 and 4,300 ft), this strange specimen looks like a many-branched candelabra. In spring its extremities sprout huge white flowers.

Death Valley

The valley was given its name by Mormon pioneers who endured unspeakable hardships when they crossed it in the 19th century. It is narrow in width but stretches more than 200 km (125 miles) in length. This area claims the lowest rainfall in the entire United States, an average of 40 mm (1.6 in) per year. In summer, true to its reputation, the valley is a veritable inferno, holding the world record for the highest average temperature—on occasion, it has reached as much as 56°C (133°F) in the shade!

The landscape, at once grandiose and desolate, glows red like a brazier at sunrise and sunset. The best places for admiring the stunning spectacle of light and shadow are Zabriskie Point and Dantes View.

On the valley floor, the salt lake of Badwater, at 86 m (282 ft) below sea-level, is the lowest point of the North American continent. The lake surface is a cracked and crumpled sheet of baked salt, which inspired some poetic soul to call it the Devil's Golf Course. The mountains which form the backdrop, snow-covered in winter, are a warren of mines.

On the western side of this national park, the ghost town of Skidoo is a relic of Gold Rush days. Near Stovepipe Wells, there are magnificent dunes to be explored. In the north, Scotty's Castle is a luxurious mansion built by an eccentric Chicago millionaire who enjoyed prospecting for gold in his spare moments.

Las Vegas

Initially a simple stagecoach stop where the Mormons built a fort, then a way-station for gold prospectors at the turn of the 20th century, Las Vegas began to develop in 1931, the year that liberal laws allowing divorce were enacted. Gaming was then introduced to enable those waiting to have their situations sorted to while away the time. But the real boom came during the post-war period. The teamsters' union invested massive funds in the gaming industry, constructing the first casino, the Flamingo, which is still going strong.

The Casinos
Ever since then, luxurious casino-hotels have been multiplying incessantly. Slot machines have invaded every corner, including the restrooms—there is said to be one per inhabitant (the population now numbers 1.5 million).

Try to arrive in Las Vegas as night falls, when the city, rising out of the desert, sparkles with ostentatious illuminations. Along Las Vegas Boulevard, nicknamed the Strip, the competition is ferocious. In an orgy of flashing neon signs, each establishment beckons customers, who total a good 30 million a year.

You owe it to yourself to visit the most extravagant casino-hotels. Among the veterans, the Circus Circus was one of the first to introduce a show: trapeze artists and other acrobats perform stunts high above the slot machines. Caesar's Palace, famous for its waitresses clad in Roman costume, has a stupendous commercial centre inspired by the colonnades of Antiquity—with talking fountains and a giant horse of Troy. Treasure Island is known for its show featuring pirates and sailors in mock battle. In the moat of the Excalibur, an Arthurian fairytale castle, a dragon spews flames. Imitation has spawned new mega-complexes whose mad decor knows no limits. The New York New York recreates all the familiar monuments of the "Big Apple": Brooklyn Bridge, the Statue of Liberty, with a roller-coaster that rattles you around Manhattan, Greenwich Village and Soho.

At the end of the Strip, some crazed engineer built the Luxor, a glass replica of the pyramid of Kheops, flanked by a life-size

New York? New York?
No, Las Vegas!

Sphinx. Inside is a miniature Nile and an exact copy of King Tut's tomb. The biggest investment of all time went into the Bellagio, a reproduction of a small Italian town on the edge of an artificial Lake Como. The casino houses a superb collection of masterpieces. The Venetian has recreated life-size replicas of Venice: St Mark's Square and the Doges' Palace, even a 356-m-long (1,200-ft) Grand Canal. The Mandalay Bay, on a Far Eastern theme, has a swimming pool with waves, a tropical sand beach around the lagoon and a shark reef that claims to hold 2,000 animals of various kinds (which you view from the shelter of a glass tunnel). The Paris Resort sports its own miniature Eiffel Tower. Among the newest hotels are the Wynn, 50 storeys high, and the South Coast, complete with equestrian centre. Look down on it all from the 360-m (1,200-ft) Stratosphere tower, which also has a casino.

The Shows

Nowadays, Las Vegas goes to great pains to ensure that its shows are geared to suit the whole family. Extravaganzas combine magic, special effects and circus acts. Year-round, celebrated international singers and bands are featured, supplemented by the occasional world-championship boxing match.

Getting Hitched

A visit to Las Vegas would not be complete without glancing into the string of wedding chapels, where for a fee of $50 to $100 you can tie the knot in just 10 minutes. For a few dollars more, they will even supply the witnesses. If you want something out of the ordinary, wed to the tune of an Elvis Presley song (impersonator included). Those who are really in a hurry can opt for the ultra-rapid drive-through version—you won't even have to leave your car!

3

THE THREE MOST SPECTACULAR CASINOS For a moment of sheer bliss, head for the **Venetian** and recapture the atmosphere of the Grand Canal, plied by gondoliers singing excerpts from operas. Don't miss the ceiling, a sumptuous depiction of a Venetian sky. At the **Bellagio**, watch the fountains playing in the lake and dream on the flower-filled verandah. Listening to the surf at **Mandalay Bay**, you can easily imagine you're being caressed by the gentle breezes of the South Seas.

The Wild West

Once you have crossed the borders of Utah or Arizona, you'll get the impression that you have entered another world. After travelling through the deserts of eastern California, you'll have grown accustomed to the limitless open spaces where the horizon melts into the sky. But in the Wild West, the light, the colours, the shapes, indeed the entire surroundings take on hitherto unimagined proportions.

The greatest concentration of national parks and nature reserves in the United States is to be found in the south of Utah and the north of Arizona, an area almost three-quarters the size of the United Kingdom. Some parks, like Grand Canyon and Monument Valley, are so famous that their name alone evokes the whole region. Others, just as spectacular, remain less familiar: Bryce Canyon and Arches, for instance.

▶ UTAH
Zion, Bryce Canyon, Capitol Reef, Arches National Park, Canyonlands, Salt Lake City

"If it's a place nobody wants, then it's the place I'm looking for" declared Brigham Young, leader of the Church of Jesus Christ of Latter-Day Saints after the death of its founder Joseph Smith. In 1847, he led his followers to the desolate lands in the north of Utah, where they settled at what is now Salt Lake City. The first years were arduous, but their unflagging efforts made the desert bloom. Today the Mormons make up almost 60 per cent of the local population. By dint of hard work and perseverance, Utah has become a rich state, but its population is still low, at just over 2.4 million. Indeed, apart from a few great industrial centres in the north, dominated by Salt Lake City, this region has largely remained an immense desert, rugged and unfit for habi-

tation, except for a few isolated river valleys. Here the cowboy is more than the stuff of legend. Some of the more spectacular and accessible landscapes are preserved in the national parks.

Zion National Park

Alluding to the mythical Jerusalem of the Mormons, Zion is a haven of sombre beauty at the heart of what was once one of the most isolated regions of the West. Carved out by the Virgin River, a tributary of the Colorado, Zion Canyon is famous for its immense walls of red sandstone, weathered by wind and water into forms of stunning grandeur.

Several trails allow you to explore the splendour of this small park; they start from a road which climbs upwards beside the tranquil river to end at the Temple of Sinawava, an area which understandably inspired awe in the Indians. Here the spectacular Narrows begin, a contraction of the canyon which forces the river between staggering walls of rock. As the first rays of the morning sun strike the rockface, the area takes on a grandiose beauty. Against the red background, white waterfalls, green junipers twisted into weird shapes by the wind and, in autumn, bright yellow foliage all make a stunning contrast. In the eastern part of the park, along Route 9, the unearthly landscape of stratified rock is dotted with isolated pinnacles.

Bryce Canyon

If the Ancients had known America, they would have included Bryce Canyon in their list of wonders of the world. Water has carved the limestone plateau into whole expanses of flamboyantly coloured pinnacles, worn by the elements into fantastic shapes. To the Paiute, they were known as "the red rocks standing like men". "A hell of a place to lose a cow!" was the less poetic description of Ebenezer Bryce, the Mormon carpenter whose name was bestowed on the canyon. The famous outlaw Butch Cassidy, a native of the area, chose this labyrinthine canyon as a safe refuge on more than one occasion.

The great organ-pipes of rock wear all the reds and oranges of the palette, shades which originate in the iron oxides and manganese present in the strata. The colours are seen to their best advantage at dawn and at dusk. In winter, a sprinkling of snow gives the summits a lacy trim.

Before arriving at Bryce, you cross Red Canyon, where rust-coloured tints dominate the scene.

Bryce Canyon looks its best when draped with a mantle of snow.

At the park entrance, the views from Sunrise or Sunset Point, and even more strikingly from Inspiration Point are staggering.

From the rocky Bryce Amphitheatre, you can walk the 9-km (5.6-mile) path of Peekaboo Loop through the national park's most beautiful area to see the Wall of Windows, the Hindu Temples and the Cathedral. The Navajo Loop, 2.5 km (1.5 miles) in length, setting out from Sunset Point, gives a good idea of the diversity of the rock formations and the natural riches of Bryce Canyon. The road (closed in winter) continues for 30 km (about 20 miles) through sagebrush, forest and meadow to Rainbow Point, offering a spectacular panorama northwards along the Pink Cliffs.

Capitol Reef

This small and little-known park is situated in ranch country about halfway between Bryce Canyon and Arches. The remains of an upthrust which occurred in an era long past, Waterpocket Fold and its intensely coloured monoliths present a gigantic open-air lesson in geology. From 100 to 200 m tall (330–660 ft), the rocks are clustered in the north of the park in Cathedral Valley. The more accessible lookout spots of Chimney Rock and Goosenecks offer fine views of these formations.

From the Visitor Center, the Scenic Drive heads out to Grand Wash, where Butch Cassidy and his gang took refuge, and then on to Capitol Gorge, at one time used by the Mormons.

Arches National Park

At the heart of the red rock region in southeast Utah near the upper Colorado River, this park contains more naturally formed arches than anywhere else in the world. The most accessible part of the park alone has more than 90 arches, produced by the particularly vigorous action of water and ice deep in the heart of the rock. Not to mention the other

GOOSENECKS

All across the West are countless canyons that rivers have carved out of the heart of the plateaux over the ages. The hazards of geology often obliged these waterways to take detours wherever the softer rock allowed their passage. In some areas, these "geological accidents" are numerous, creating a succession of erratic twists and turns that local people refer to as *goosenecks*. A fascinating example can be seen near Mexican Hat in Utah, where the loops of the San Juan River bend so much that they seem to intersect.

ARCHES NATIONAL PARK • CANYONLANDS

Wind and rain have carved this astonishing Utah landscape of arches and balancing rocks.

strange formations that have been created by erosion, including boulders precariously balanced on pinnacles.

It is in fact Balanced Rock which opens the trail to the Windows section, where the powerful silhouettes of a group of eight monumental arches—including a double arch—stand stark against the sky.

Further on, another trail leads to a view of Delicate Arch, perhaps the most beautiful of all. A moderately strenuous climb takes you close up to the arch, but it appears more impressive from below, seemingly teetering on the edge of a cliff.

Devil's Garden, in the north of the park, has the largest cluster of arches. A 12-km (8-mile) loop, varying from easy to strenuous, leads you past Pine Tree, Partition, Double O, Dark Angel and Landscape arches, this last being the longest formation of its type in the world.

Canyonlands

This immense national park spread either side of the Green River before it joins the Colorado, is one of the least-visited in the West, probably because it is often accessible only by four-wheel drive. Canyonlands is remarkable for the diversity of its

> **CORAL-PINK SAND DUNES**
>
> A little before Kanab and about 15 km (9 miles) south of Route 89, beautiful tawny sand dunes ripple over a wide plateau. This geological phenomenon is the accumulation, over many thousands of years, of particles of eroded red sandstone, swept by powerful winds through a gap between the Moquith and Moccasin mountains.

rock formations, from afar like great, crumbling fortresses, in a riotous medley of colours and configurations—flat-topped mesas, spires, pinnacles, mushrooms, arches and canyons.

The park is divided into three zones: the west, called the Maze, inaccessible to ordinary cars; the north, which boasts breathtaking views from Dead Horse State Park and Grandview Point; and the south or Needles district, where the scenery comes straight out of a Western, approached by Route 211. On the way, stop off at Newspaper Rock, a wall of rock etched with Indian petroglyphs. Indeed, there are many vestiges of its Native American past in the park.

Salt Lake City

The capital of the Mormon state and Church is clean, spacious and orderly. When Salt Lake City was chosen as the site for the Winter Olympics of 2002, television stations broadcast worldwide the celebrations that took place on Temple Square, dominated by the Mormon Temple. Next door to this 19th-century church, topped by no less than six steeples, the Tabernacle boasts a celebrated choir of more than 300 voices. Even taller than the Temple, the modern Latter Day Saints Church Office Building is world headquarters of the Mormon Church. Guided tours take you up close to the sacred precincts and afford a glimpse into Mormon religious practice.

Although the town is full of statues and monuments, none is more eloquent than the seagull monument standing in the shadow of the Temple: a perpetual tribute to the gulls nesting on the islands of the Great Salt Lake, which saved the harvest in the settlement's early days by devouring a swarm of locusts.

Great Salt Lake

In the middle of the desert, 32 km (20 miles) west of the city, lies the Great Salt Lake, thick with minerals surpassed in salinity only by the Dead Sea. It's easy enough to float in, if you don't object to being caked in salt; the problem is getting yourself upright again.

ARIZONA
Indian Corner, Page and Lake Powell, Grand Canyon, Flagstaff Region, Phoenix, Tucson, Ghost Towns

Arizona, in all its glory, will not disappoint you. Once seen, the landscapes are unforgettable, and here you will encounter Indians, now, in these politically correct days, called Native Americans. In the north, on lands more than twice the size of Wales, 200,000 Navajo have preserved their culture to a large extent. They manage some of the most famous Arizona sites, including Monument Valley. Southern Arizona offers a different image: dominated by the Sonora Desert, it bristles with cactus and its towns are ghosts. Because of its beauty, or the warmth of its sun, Arizona has the most rapidly growing population of all American states.

Indian Corner

The northeast corner of Arizona is the exclusive domain of Native American tribes. Distributed across three states, but primarily in Arizona, the Navajo now form the largest tribe in the United States. Threatened by extinction in 1864, then deported into the middle of the desert, they finally obtained from the American government their own territory. Initially numbering no more than 10,000, they have progressively built up their community, and now the tide has turned. The Navajo reservation has become an autonomous nation within the framework of the federal government. Wary but well-organized, their pride recovered, the people are in control of their future. They may have integrated something of the cowboy folklore into their culture, but of all the ethnic groups it is the Navajo that most determinedly hands down its traditions from one generation to the next. Sand painting, dancing and the cult of the hallucinogenic *peyotl* are still commonly practised.

All the tribes of northern Arizona, beginning with the Hopi, are now claiming their identity. The new industries of tourism, gambling and mining as well as cattle farming, to a lesser extent, have meant that fewer of the native peoples need to be exiled to the towns.

Monument Valley

At the end of the 1930s, Hollywood practically took over the heart of Navajo country. Every Western was filmed against a backdrop of jagged rock buttes silhouetted on the horizon. The

> **THE NAVAJO CODE**
> During World War II, the Americans discovered the ultimate weapon in the battle for the airwaves. To ensure that neither the Japanese nor the Germans could intercept their radio messages, they put the Navajo in charge of broadcasting. The Navajo language, unwritten, structurally complicated, never the object of study, was impossible to decipher. In all, 400 Amerindians served in the Navajo Code Talker Corps.

sandstone towers were those of Monument Valley. According to a gruesome Navajo legend, the mesas of the valley are the scattered body parts of a murderous giant who was tortured then chopped up into pieces.

The image may be macabre but it is in some ways realistic. An uplifted plateau forged by erosion, Monument Valley is dotted with haphazard groups of strangely shaped towers. Totem Pole, for example, seems to defy the laws of gravity, remaining upright only by miracle.

As everywhere in the West, sunrise and sunset tint the landscape with the most beautiful hues, in all the shades from pink to dark violet. The best viewpoint is probably the one from the Visitor Center.

A rough track runs through the valley, which is peopled by Navajo who subsist by agriculture and sheep-farming. The flocks make a magnificent picture against a background of amber-coloured hills. The Navajo still live in the traditional *hogan*, a round hut of wood and clay.

Navajo Monument

Between Monument Valley and Lake Powell, a small park contains the ruins of two 13th-century Indian villages. Navajo Monument is one of three main sites of the Anasazi culture, a little-known tribe which became extinct in the 13th century and whose descendants are the Hopi Indians.

First nomads, then farmers after the discovery of maize, the Anasazi lived in the canyons where they cultivated their crops on terraces. Their villages were sheltered by cliff overhangs, which explains their extraordinary state of preservation.

Easily reached by a short footpath, an overlook allows you to peer into the ruins of Betatakin at the bottom of a hollow of the Tsegi Canyon, a settlement which once numbered 100 inhabitants. The site can only be visited with a ranger. The round trip is 8 km (5 miles) in all, and you should allow five hours. Another footpath leads to the more distant

INDIAN CORNER

ruins of Keet Seel, where the journey there and back covers 26 km (16 miles).

Chelly Canyon

At the eastern edge of Arizona, near the border with New Mexico, this Navajo tribal park encompasses two deep canyons: the Chelly Canyon itself and the Canyon del Muerto (in the north). There are more than 60 ruined Indian villages, dating from 350 to 1300. The most beautiful of these is at White House, right in the canyon. A handful of well-preserved dwellings cluster together at the foot of a sheer red cliff. Allow two hours for the round trip along an easy footpath. Shortly before arriving at the village, you have to wade twice across the shallow Chelly River. The Navajo guardians usually build a bridge of branches for the second crossing.

As at many other places in the park, Navajo families set up camp for the summer on the floor of the canyon where their animals can graze. Some cultivate small fields.

With the exception of White House, it is forbidden to hike alone in the park. You will need to sign up for a guided tour to visit the well-preserved sites of the Canyon del Muerto (Antelope House and Mummy Cave), to admire the magnificent Spider Rock overlook from the end of the road, or to view the petroglyphs covering the canyon walls (such as at Standing Cow Ruin).

> **ON TOP WITH THE HOPI**
> Perched on the summits of three mesas, the Hopi adobe villages form an enclave in Navajo territory. Numbering only 18,000, the Hopi worship a vast pantheon of gods through *kachinas*, wooden dolls representing the spirits. Their colourful dances, consecrated to the snake, the butterfly, the *kachina*, and so on, are frequently performed in summer. Hopi crafts, in particular pottery, are of remarkable quality.

Petrified Forest

The Petrified Forest National Park, 35 km (22 miles) east of Holbrook, protects a vast area covered by fossilized tree trunks. At the end of the tertiary era, more than 5 million years ago, the rivers deposited fallen trees in a sedimentary basin. Thanks to a coating of silt that guarded them from the elements, the trees did not decompose. They were eventually turned to stone by a volcanic eruption which scattered ash containing silica all over the area, the subsequent chemical reaction fossilizing the trees.

ARIZONA

> **METEORITE CRATER**
> Between Flagstaff and the Petrified Forest, in the middle of the desert, is the world's biggest meteorite crater, its diameter exceeding 1,200 m (3,900 ft) and with a maximum depth of 175 m (574 ft). In the museum at the crater's edge, you will learn how the impact must have corresponded to a meteorite of more than 10 million tons.

Much later, erosion stripped away the top soil, and the petrified forest was exposed to view. Some of the trunks are vividly coloured, with blue, orange and red tints. The greatest concentrations of petrified trees are to be found at Long Logs and at Giant Logs in the south section of the park, and there are many other fossilized logs at Crystal Ford.

In the north, do not miss the intense and varied colours of the Painted Desert, best at sunset.

Page and Lake Powell

The enormous cliffs of red sandstone rising from the midnight-blue waters of Lake Powell make a striking picture. This immense and labyrinthine stretch of water, 300 km (186 miles) long and covering an area of 5,000 sq km (nearly 2,000 sq miles), was the by-product of the Glen Canyon Dam, built on the Colorado River in the late 1950s. The lake has given its name to a vast national park. Its convoluted shoreline is frilled by no less than 96 canyons, which look rather like fjords.

Page is a small resort at the extreme west of the lake; the visitor centre is housed in the John Wesley Powell Memorial Museum. From Page, follow the road over the dam to the Wahweap marina. Hiring a boat is definitely the best way of discovering the full majesty of Lake Powell. Rainbow Bridge is a monumental natural arch on the bank at the foot of Navajo Mountain, accessible by boat, on foot, or on horseback. Powerboats, personal watercraft and kayaks are available for short rental, or you can rent a houseboat. Alternatively, you can join a full- or half-day excursion.

Many Indian sites are scattered throughout the region. The most interesting, associated with the Anasazi, are at Iceberg Canyon near the Escalante River.

Of course, you can always spend a day swimming and lazing by the lake. There are several pleasant beaches by the marina, and in summer the water warms up to 26°C (79°F).

Antelope Canyon: one of Mother Nature's most spectacular works of art.

Antelope Canyon

Not to be missed, this slot canyon is located in the Navajo reservation off Route 98 as you leave Page. Gouged out by a seasonal tributary of the Colorado River, Antelope Canyon has water-weathered walls that a sculptor might envy. The rock face surges and swells like waves, and at midday the sun reaches in to throw the geometrical stripes of the walls into brilliant relief. The play of light and shadow on the orange-brown walls is indescribably beautiful. You have to pay a fee to gain access to the canyon, which is located on Navajo territory. If you don't have a four-wheel drive vehicle, an Indian guide will take you to the canyon for $15.

Marble Canyon

Downriver from Lake Powell and the Glen Canyon Dam, the Colorado River carves its way between steep cliffs. About 60 km (38 miles) south of Page, Route 89A (leading to the north side of the Grand Canyon) brings you to what was until the end of the 19th century the only river crossing at Lee's Ferry. From here the first ferry sailed from Arizona to Utah at the end of the 19th century. Thousands of young Mormon couples travelled this way to get married in Utah, earning it the name Honeymoon Trail. Lee's Ferry is today a favourite departure point for rafting enthusiasts. By descending the Colorado, you can penetrate to the very heart of the canyon, which you can otherwise only touch on.

Grand Canyon

The Grand Canyon of the Colorado is indeed the grandest of them all. Nothing else on earth can compare: its shape, dimensions, colours, topography, everything about it is bigger, more

4

THE FOUR BEST SLOT CANYONS In Arizona, Nature has let her imagination run wild. Carved into the red rock by the seasonal waters of tributaries of the Colorado River, the narrow canyons of **Antelope**, **Johnson**, **Pariah** and **Tao**, in places only a few feet wide, are true wonders of the world. To walk through them when the water is low at the end of spring or in autumn is an unforgettable experience.

GRAND CANYON

beautiful than anywhere else. And when you see it "for real", you'll find it a hundred times more impressive than anything you might have imagined or seen in photographs.

The formation of the Grand Canyon is a perfect object lesson in river erosion. The Colorado River has been carving out its bed for almost a billion years, wearing through the various layers of sedimentary rock deposited since the beginning of time. Right down at the bottom of the chasm are the most ancient rocks, hard, shiny black Precambrian schist and gneiss, the oldest exposed rocks on earth. On top of them is a layer of sandstone, then green shale, brown limestone and a thin layer of sandstone. Above that, a deposit of grey-blue limestone contains traces of amphibian and fern fossils, enabling it to be dated at 265 million years old. This is coloured with red streaks from the iron oxides washed down from the beds above— shale and sandstone, probably deposited at the end of the Palaeozoic era. Next comes a layer of soft shaly rock known as Hermit shale, and above that, Coconino sandstone, 190 million years old, the solidified remains of sand dunes in which fossilized footprints indicate lizard life. At the top is the pale grey Kaibab limestone, riddled with fossils of creatures that dwelt in a shallow sea 180 million years ago— sponges, sharks' teeth, corals and bivalves.

The maximum depth reaches 1,600 m (5,200 ft). Because of the differences of altitude, there are no less than five different types of climate in the Grand Canyon, ranging from the semi-desert of the floor to the Arctic chill at the tops of the flanking mountains. Whereas the North Rim, much higher and cooler, is snow-covered in winter, the South Rim has very little snow and the floor of the gorge never so much as a flake. The fauna and flora are consequently greatly varied. The North Rim is covered with pines while the natural vegetation of the South is dwarf junipers and succulents, and the canyon bottom is home to iguanas and rattlesnakes.

Generally visitors only explore one side; as the crow flies, the two rims are close together, but the road from south to north is more than 300 km (186 miles) in length.

South Rim

Less than two hours by road from Flagstaff, the South Rim is more accessible than the North. The film shown at the IMAX Theatre at Grand Canyon Village is a good half-hour introduction to the canyon, the life of the Anasazi who lived there 4,000 years ago, and the men who braved the rapids.

Walkers and hikers have to call in at the Backcountry Office in Grand Canyon Village to pick up a permit. From there, two scenic paths offer the best panoramas of the canyon. The much longer eastern path, known as Cameron Road, is open to vehicles, stretching for 45 km (28 miles) as far as Desert View. It includes several viewing areas which are superb at sunset: Mather Point (also accessible on foot from the Visitor Center by the Rim Trail), Yaki Point, Grand View Point and Lipan Point, from where you can see the meanders of the Colorado which are otherwise hidden from view.

The western path, 11 km (7 miles) long, can only be covered on foot or by the shuttle bus which leaves approximately every 15 minutes. Viewed from Maricopa and Hopi Points, sunrise and sunset are out of this world. A little further on, the Abyss lookout dominates the canyon from a height of 900 m (3,000 ft). West Rim Drive ends at Hermit's Rest. The path from Trail View Overlook to the Village is the most frequented in the park. It descends to Indian Gardens, a small oasis on an intermediate plateau, and then all the way down to the Colorado River. It is possible to hike, allowing one long day to reach Indian Gardens and return, and two days for the round trip to the river and back. You can also do this excursion by mule, but you must reserve long in advance.

North Rim

Only 10 per cent of visitors to the Grand Canyon go to the North Rim because it is rather isolated. Access is from Utah or by way of Page and Lake Powell. Notwithstanding, this side offers views of the Canyon every bit as fine as those from the South Rim.

From the road on the north side, which follows the contours of the Whalala Plateau, the views beyond the spruce forests at Point Imperial, Angel Window and Cape Royal are particularly magnificent when bathed in the light of the setting sun. Even better is the panorama from Point Sublime, the closest to the gorge and accessible by way of a track—but take care in wet weather!

If you like hiking, note that the path from Bright Angel Point leads to the bottom of the canyon and then climbs to Grand Canyon Village on the South Rim. You should allow at least two days for this trip.

The incomparable Grand Canyon, etched by the Colorado River.

> **SKYWALK**
> If you're not afraid of heights, go for a walk in the sky over the Grand Canyon. Opened in 2007 by the Hualapai Indian tribe at Eagle Point, the Skywalk is a horseshoe-shaped glass platform anchored to the ledge, perched more than 1,200 m (4,000 ft) above the canyon floor and jutting over 20 m (65 ft) into the void. Transport is by bus, operated by the Hualapai, and no photographs are allowed.

About 150 km (94 miles) downriver, the Toroweap Overlook is reached by a dirt road 110 km (69 miles) long: from Route 389, 15 km (10 miles) west of Fredonia, follow the signs for Grand Canyon National Monument and Tuweep. This must be the most grandiose panorama of the entire canyon: sheer cliffs plunge down to the Colorado, lying 900 m (3,000 ft) below. The light of the rising sun on these cliff walls is incredibly beautiful.

The overlooks on the North Rim are generally inaccessible from October to May because of snow. At all times the unsurfaced roads are difficult to negotiate.

Havasupai

Some 50 km (30 miles) from Grand Canyon Village as the crow flies, the Havasupai Reservation is the preserve of one of the smallest tribes in the United States (550 individuals). It has only one village, Supai, reached by foot or on horseback from the end of the road at Hualalai Hilltop. Clustered round an oasis, the village (which has a hotel and camp site) is famous for its magnificent waterfalls and pools of turquoise water studding the Havasu River. To reserve, contact Havasupai Tourist Enterprises, Supai, AZ 86435.

Flagstaff Region

Within a radius of about 50 km (30 miles) around Flagstaff, gateway to northern Arizona, are several places of interest. Flagstaff itself isn't particularly impressive, apart from its small Museum of Northern Arizona, devoted to Native American cultures.

Oak Creek Canyon

This spectacular gorge, 26 km (16 miles) from Flagstaff, is justly famous for its colourful crumbling pillars of rock surrounded by pine forest. Numerous Westerns have been filmed here.

Sedona

Further south, Sedona is a pleasant town ringed by red mountains (Red Rock Crossing), known for its art galleries and artists' studios (painter Max Ernst lived here). To New Age adepts it is a "sacred energy area". The Tlaquepaque district has been remodelled in Mexican style. In the vicinity, the small Red Rock Park abounds in weird rock formations, specially intense in colour. Near the entrance is a rock with a hole through the middle.

Montezuma Castle

Situated close to the Phoenix Highway, just after the turn-off for Sedona, this very beautiful five-storey Indian village ruin clinging to the hillside overlooks the valley floor from a height of 30 m (98 ft). A natural fortress and still 90 per cent intact, the cliff-dwelling is one of the best-preserved in all the Southwest. When it was inhabited, the only way into or out of the village, either from above or below, was by means of ladders, a somewhat perilous approach. Remains of similar settlements of great interest are scattered all over the region, for example at Walnut Canyon, Sinagua Indian Ruins and Wupatki Monument.

Phoenix

In the middle of the desert, Phoenix is the capital of Arizona with 3.7 million inhabitants. It spreads over a very large area, a city where the suburbs are the centre of life. America's senior citizens come here in droves, drawn by the perpetual sunshine and warm climate. The same is true of Sun City, 27 km (17 miles) away, where there's hardly anyone under the age of 60. Even the policemen and aerobics teachers have grey hair. The centre of Phoenix, discreet and airy, bristles with skyscrapers.

Museums

The Heard Museum (2301 N Central Ave) provides an informative introduction to the different Native American cultures of the Southwest, including a fascinating collection of *kachina* dolls, some of them donated by senator Barry Goldwater. Performances of Indian dances or demonstrations of Indian crafts are held at weekends.

At 1625 N Central Avenue, the Phoenix Art Museum has a number of eclectic collections, from pre-Columbian and Asian art to classical painting and modern art.

In Patago Park, 1201 N Galvin Parkway, the Desert Botanical Garden groups all the plant species native to southern Arizona. The neighbouring Hall of Flame is the biggest museum in the world entirely devoted to the fire service.

Scottsdale

An elegant residential suburb of Phoenix, Scottsdale has dozens of

ARIZONA

The Arizona desert is far from barren: cacti flourish in the heat.

galleries clustered in an intimate, arty district. In addition to the Buffalo Museum of America (10261 N Scottsdale Road), there are various themed malls, for instance Borgata, a reconstruction of an Italian 16th-century village.

On the heights, you can visit Taliesin West, which houses the foundation of the celebrated architect Frank Lloyd Wright, inventor of the "natural house", a dwelling that blends into its environment, and designer of the New York Guggenheim Museum.

Prescott

Nestling in the hills and surrounded by lakes, Prescott preserves some old buildings dating from its days as an old mining town. The Smoki Museum has an interesting collection of Indian artefacts.

Tucson

Like Phoenix, the dynamic city of Tucson rises out of the Sonora Desert. Ringed by mountains, the ancient Spanish town has largely given way to a flourishing financial quarter studded with skyscrapers. Nevertheless, there is still a good deal of Mexican influence here, and the frontier is only about 100 km (63 miles) away. The places of interest are out of the town centre.

San Xavier Mission
To the south, in the Indian reservation of San Xavier, the mission of the same name dates from the end of the 18th century. It is one of the finest in the West, in typical Hispanic style. The mission is known as the "Desert Dove" and harbours relics which feature in the annual festival honouring the Virgin of Guadalupe.

Biosphere-2
Some 50 km (30 miles) north of Tucson, on the western slopes of Mount Lemmon (along Route 77), Biosphere-2 is the home of one of the better-known and more controversial scientific experiments of recent years. Along with thousands of species of plants and animals, a team of researchers lived entirely self-sufficiently for two years under a vast Plexiglass bubble, having no physical contact with the external world. They emerged in September 1993, thinner but maybe wiser than before. No one is locked inside the bubble any more, but you can tour the installations where scientific experiments are still performed.

Tucson Mountain Park
West of town, this park contains the Old Tucson theme park and the admirable Arizona-Sonora Desert Museum, where, in the Earth Sciences Center, you can learn about the history and geology of the area and observe endearing creatures like tarantulas and rattlesnakes. Outside, in simulated natural habitats, are mountain lions and jaguars and other injured animals rescued from the desert. The cactus garden is planted with virtually every species of cactus, including the rarest and the most beautiful, bursting into bloom in spring. There is also an aviary with hummingbirds and a cave dripping with stalactites.

Old Tucson is a movie set rehabilitated as an amusement park. It represents a typical frontier town with saloon, bank, jail, rail station, Chinese quarter and so forth. Part of *Rio Bravo* was filmed here and *Gunfight at the O.K. Corral* completed. To the right of the entrance, the names of all the stars who have played here are carved on the planks of the sidewalk. At fixed times, actors replay gunfights from the best-known films.

Saguaro National Monument
One part east and one part west of Tucson, Saguaro Park is the only place on earth where the giant saguaro cactus grows, proliferating on the rocky outcrops of the Tucson hills. Branching into huge candelabra—they can develop 50 branches or more—the saguaro is the biggest cactus in the

world. It frequently reaches 12 m (40 ft) in height and can live for 200 years. When rain falls in the region in summer—a rare occurrence—the saguaro's complex root system can suck up as much as a ton of water in a few minutes. Its trunk is pitted with woodpecker holes, and tiny owls, only a few inches long, nest in its branches.

The saguaro flowers in June, releasing 12 million seeds. On average, only one from each plant will germinate and survive to produce a mature plant. In summer the cactus produces fruit, from which the Papago Indians of the Sonora Desert make jam and even alcohol.

The best time to visit the park is from March to July, when the wildflowers blossom and the many species of cactus also flower.

Organ Pipe

Less well-known than Saguaro, Organ Pipe Cactus National Monument lies along the Mexican frontier, halfway between Tucson and California. UNESCO has declared this park an "international biosphere reserve". More than 30 different varieties of cactus grow here in addition to the organ pipe, which can reach 6 to 7 m (20–23 ft) in height and blooms around the month of May. The park includes an unspoilt area of the Sonora Desert where animal life flourishes. Birds are particularly numerous here, both in winter and at the migratory season.

Two dirt roads lead into the park: Ajo Mountain Loop and Puerto Blanco Drive, passing by the Quitobaquito Oasis. A footpath near the Visitor Center concentrates much of the flora of the region into one short walk.

5

THE FIVE MOST GORGEOUS SUNSETS In the West, sunlight is the supreme artist, breathing life into the most grandiose of views. The setting of the sun on the Grand Canyon, seen from the South Rim at **Yaki Point** or, even better, from the North Rim at **Toroweap Point**, is a spectacle of unrivalled splendour. Similarly, on no account should you miss the burnished beauty of **Monument Valley**, **Bryce Canyon** or **Zion**, where the rocks at sundown radiate a unique coral glow.

Ghost Towns

More than a dozen of these abandoned towns are scattered across southeast Arizona. Some, such as Gleeson, Charleston, Pearce or Washington Camp, have all but vanished. There is nothing left but a name on the map and a few tumbledown buildings battered by the winds. On the other hand, two have survived the closing of the turquoise, gold, copper and silver mines. These are Bisbee and Tombstone, wallowing in nostalgia.

Bisbee

Situated in a hollow of the Mule Mountains on the threshold of Mexico, this ex-mining town has been turned over to tourism. Built on terraces, it is served by a network of stepped alleyways. You can visit its Lavender Pit, an open-cast mine, and the galleries of the Queen Copper Mine.

In town, the old Copper Queen Hotel brings back memories of early Westerns, and the renovated Victorian buildings of the centre evoke an atmosphere of times past.

Tombstone

A short distance to the north, Tombstone stands testimony to its motto—"the town too tough to die". It was founded by a pessimistic prospector who had been heard to lament that the only thing he would find in the area would be his own tombstone. An old mining town, Tombstone had a reputation for violence at the time of the conquest of the West. A number of buildings dating from those days have now been restored.

Saloons and stores line up behind their wooden façades all along the main street. Near the old courthouse are the offices of the local newspaper, *The Epitaph*. Tombstone is famous for being the scene of the original duel featured in the film *Gunfight at the O.K. Corral*.

At the northern exit of town, a small cemetery contains the graves of the desperados who died in droves during the 1880s when Tombstone was at the height of its glory. Among the graphic epitaphs you'll read "killed by X in the street at Tombstone", "lynched", "stabbed to death", "killed by Indians", "legally hanged", and so on.

In just one weekend, you can relive the feverish days of the close of the 19th century. The people of Tombstone don their costumes and offer stagecoach rides, or even a hanging in the town square! In October, during the Helldorado Days, the whole town steps back a hundred years and becomes the setting for hilarious mock shoot-outs and lynchings in the middle of the street.

NEW MEXICO AND COLORADO
Albuquerque, Santa Fe, Taos, Indian Villages, Mesa Verde, Durango, Silverton

It was on their quest to find the mythical Eldorado (so mythical that nobody ever discovered it) that the Spanish began their colonization of the American Southwest. Santa Fe, founded in 1609, became capital of the colonies of this part of the New World, and New Mexico was the spearhead of the pacification and conversion of the Indians, who resisted as best they could, though they were widely dispersed. It wasn't until the middle of the 19th century, after the newly independent Mexico was defeated, that the vast territories of New Mexico, Arizona and California came under American domination.

At the foot of the Rocky Mountains, the state of Colorado was formed, joining the Union in 1876. More unstable, New Mexico, situated beyond its southern border, had to wait till 1912 before it could achieve the status of state.

A mountainous territory, Colorado covers an area of 269,500 sq km (104,000 sq miles), about half the size of France, and has a population of 4 million, half of whom live in greater Denver. New Mexico, a region of high plateaux and desert, is less densely populated: 1.7 million inhabitants for an area of 315,000 sq km (121,600 sq miles). Nearly four centuries after its foundation, the state has retained a rich cultural heritage from its turbulent past. Its Native American origins can be found in the oldest settlements on the continent; the Indian villages are lively and the traditional dances have been maintained. The Spanish heritage is evident in the architecture of the old towns, the strong Catholic influence and large Mexican community, which represents 30 per cent of the population.

Albuquerque

The little colony founded in 1706 and named after the Duke of Albuquerque, Viceroy of New Spain, has grown today into the biggest town in New Mexico. It is famous for its annual hot-air balloon festival, the biggest in the world, when enthusiasts descend on the town in droves. At the meeting point of the Hispanic and Native American worlds, this prosperous city is justly proud of its cultural heritage.

Native peoples celebrate their traditions in modern-day pow-wows.

The Plaza

The city's nerve centre is the Old Town, the old Spanish heart of the city, and more specifically around the central plaza, dominated by the twin-towered adobe church of San Felipe de Neri. The surrounding ochre and adobe streets have been smartened up but still recall the past, not without making some concessions to the present—restaurants, art galleries, craft and souvenir shops abound. West of the plaza, the Rattlesnake Museum is full of live exhibits.

At 1801 Mountain Road NW, the Museum of Natural History and Science is devoted to the fauna and geology of the region and displays a collection of dinosaur skeletons, a simulated volcanic eruption and the replica of an Ice Age snow cave. At No. 2000, the Albuquerque Museum of Art and History documents its early Native American inhabitants and Spanish colonizers (weapons, artefacts).

The Pueblo Center

Further north, the fascinating Indian Pueblo Cultural Center (2401 12th Street NW), housed in a building of Indian design, is a must. Inside, you'll learn everything there is to know about the Pueblo tribes of New Mexico, both ancient and modern. Jewellery, costumes, pottery and photos help to identify the different groups. Traditional dances and displays of arts and crafts take place on weekends.

The Surroundings

The campus of the University of New Mexico, east of the town, is the site of several other museums: geology, biology, art (mainly of Spanish origin) and anthropology. There is even a museum devoted exclusively to meteorites.

At the western exit of Albuquerque, the Petroglyph National Monument preserves thousands of drawings carved out of the rock by the ancestors of the Pueblo Indians from the 14th century onwards.

Sandia Crest to the north is a very popular destination, reached by the Sandia Peak Aerial Tram, which claims to be the world's longest single-span tramway. From the summit, a network of paths provide plenty of opportunities for walking or mountain biking. In winter, the mountains form a vast ski area.

Santa Fe

The second-oldest city in the United States, founded by the Spanish in 1609, even before the first permanent English colony on the East Coast, Santa Fe has retained a timeless charm, and is unique in North America. The

SANTA FE

Adobe houses in Santa Fe, an architecture that is both resistant and elegant.

conquistadors borrowed from the Pueblo Indians the design of their low flat-roofed adobe dwellings, which are still the rule here. The old buildings around the central plaza and along the narrow streets offer a harmonious architectural unity. Although the atmosphere is still impregnated with strong Indian and Spanish influences, modernity has not bypassed Santa Fe. Many old houses have been converted into shops and art galleries, and dozens of artists, drawn to Santa Fe by its particular atmosphere, have settled in the area. Inevitably, an ever-increasing stream of tourists have followed in their footsteps, making the capital of New Mexico one of the country's most visited cities.

The Plaza

Santa Fe was the last stop on the famous Santa Fe Trail, which linked the city to Missouri, and in the Spanish colonial days the plaza was the market place. On the west side rises the Palace of the Governors, one of the town's earliest buildings (1610–14). It was the residence of a succession of Spanish, Mexican and American governors and served as the capitol after the 1860s. The oldest building in continual use in the United States, it houses today a museum tracing the history of the region, with fine Indian and Spanish collections. Next door, the Fine Arts Museum is devoted to 20th-century New Mexican art. Farther west, on Johnson Street, the Georgia O'Keeffe Museum pays tribute to this famous American painter. She lived for many years near Santa Fe, and died here in 1986, aged 99.

East of the Plaza, the Institute of American Indian Arts Museum is devoted exclusively to modern Amerindian art. Next door, St Francis Cathedral was built in the 19th century by the French archbishop Lamy. Inside, in the chapel of Our Lady of the Rosary, is the oldest wooden statue of the Virgin in North America. She was sculpted in Mexico and brought to Santa Fe in 1625. Legend has it that she helped the Spanish recapture the town in 1692 after they were driven out by the Indians.

Just north of the main plaza, Sena Plaza was once the central courtyard of a large hacienda. It has been converted into a secluded garden, perfect if you need some peace and quiet in beautiful surroundings.

The Southern Districts

Along the old Santa Fe Trail, the 19th-century Loreto Chapel is renowned for its remarkable stone spiral staircase built with no nails or obvious signs of support, and known as the "Miraculous Staircase". According to legend it was built by a travelling carpenter who disappeared as soon as the stairs were built. It's said he was none other than St Joseph.

South of the Río is the Analco district, site of Santa Fe's oldest house (dating from 1200), today a souvenir shop, and the San Miguel Chapel, the oldest church in the United States. It was built in 1610–1625 and remodelled several times. To the east, Canyon Road and its surrounding streets, formerly an artists' haunt, now boast numerous upmarket galleries.

Further south, beyond Capitol, a huge complex combines several museums on the Camino Lejo. The Museum of Indian Arts and Culture, which houses the collections of the Laboratory of Anthropology, is devoted to the costumes and crafts of the different tribes of the Southwest. One of the best is the Museum of International Folk Art, which, as its name suggests, presents the folklore of dozens of countries. In addition, it has an excellent section of Hispanic art, including the magnificent works of popular art in the Girard collection.

The Wheelwright Museum displays Indian art, both ancient and modern, enhanced by fascinating exhibitions devoted in particular to the Navajos.

To the southwest of town, at the intersection of Guadalupe and Agua Fria, is the oldest adobe church in the Southwest. Built at the end of the 18th century, it is dedicated to the Virgin of Guadalupe, patron saint of Mexico. Concerts are regularly held here.

Taos

Set on the edge of an Indian reserve of the same name, the little town of Taos was founded by a group of Spanish settlers in 1615, a few years after Santa Fe. It suffered from repercussions of the great Pueblo Revolt of 1680, because of its proximity to the Taos Pueblo, established nearly 1,000 years ago. A succession of troubles followed its passing under American rule, and the town—renowned for its magical light— was ushered into the 20th century with the arrival of numerous painters and writers, among them Georgia O'Keefe and D.H. Lawrence (whose ashes are enshrined at a ranch 20 miles northwest of town). The bohemian tradition still lingers, judging by the host of art galleries and museums crowding its narrow streets. But most of the hippies that came to the region in the 1960s have packed their bags and gone, and Taos remains more authentic and less tourist-oriented than Santa Fe. The surroundings lend themselves to all kinds of sports, from winter skiing in the Taos Valley to rafting and hiking in the warmer months.

Downtown

Here again, the town revolves around its plaza, surrounded by pretty adobe houses. On the north side is the residence of the first American governor of the territory, Charles Bent, which has been turned into a museum. Its owner was killed and scalped by the Indians in 1847 during the revolt against American control. Near the esplanade, the home of the famous pioneer Kit Carson, who acted as a scout during the Indian wars, is also a museum. The interior is typical of the 1830s and 1840s, furnished with all the accoutrements of the trappers and settlers of the time.

The homes of a colourful array of artists who set up shop in Taos have been turned into museums. Among them, look out for the 1797 house of the painter Blumenschein at 222 Ledoux Street, and the Harwood Foundation, a small museum of local art. At No. 227 Pueblo Norte, the Fechin Institute blends the pueblo style of Taos with the sculptures of its former Russian occupant.

The Surroundings

Don't miss a visit to the Hacienda de los Martinez, a huge windowless pile 3 km (less than 2 miles) west of the plaza. At the end of the 18th century, local inhabitants took refuge with their livestock in the fortified building to escape Comanche or Apache raids. Today it is a museum devoted to Spanish colonial life.

South of the town, at Ranchos de Taos, the adobe church of San Francisco de Asis dates from the same period. Topped by twin steeples, it is one of the prettiest churches in the American West.

Going north this time, you'll come to the Millicent Rogers Museum—on the street of the same name—housing the wealthy heiress's magnificent personal collection. She was fascinated by Spanish colonial and Indian art. The section devoted to Maria Martinez, who breathed new life into Pueblo pottery, is outstanding. Superb *kachinas* (Hopi ritual dolls), costumes and jewellery are also on view, not to mention a section of contemporary Amerindian art.

Some 20 km (12 miles) from Taos, an impressive bridge straddles the Rio Grande gorge—the second biggest suspension bridge in the United States. The view over the river and sides of the gorge is spectacular.

Taos Pueblo

This pueblo village situated only 5 km (3 miles) northeast of Taos was one of the most important Indian centres in the Southwest, until the arrival of the Spanish. Its exact origins have been lost in the mists of time, but its inhabitants maintain they have been here for at least 1,000 years. The village of adobe dwellings has a superb architectural harmony. The several hundred residents live without electricity or running water. You can walk freely around a small section of the village during the daytime or join a guided tour, which will provide an interesting insight into the world of the Pueblos.

In addition to the galleries displaying works by Indian painters, you will see the central plaza traversed by a stream, with its pair of churches, fortified dwellings and two huge four- and five-storey communal houses. Be aware that Taos is closed for several weeks of the year during the traditional ceremonies. It is, however, open to the public for the spectacular Feast of San Geronimo, held in the last few days of September.

Indian Pueblos

The cool high plateaux of the New Mexican northwest form a region that stands somewhat apart from the rest of the American landscape. In addition to Spanish colonial towns, you'll come across dozens of small Indian pueblos, some that have been

INDIAN PUEBLOS

Traditional Indian motifs appear on everything from pottery to house walls.

lying in ruins for several centuries, others that could hardly be livelier. They are spread out over several reservations and beyond: Isleta, Canoncito, Laguna, Acoma, Navajo and Zuni to the west of Albuquerque; San Felipe, Santa Ana, Zia, Santo Domingo, Jemez Springs, Taos and Apaches Jicarillas to the north. Although some pueblos have cast aside the traditional way of life and opened their own casinos, in most of them people still live according to the "old ways". While many have grouped together to promote themselves, with Visitor Centers arranging guided tours around several pueblos at a time, some are off-limits during ritual ceremonies, and photography may be forbidden on certain occasions.

West of Albuquerque

The small Laguna reserve, reputed for its many festivals, groups six villages. Various Indian tribes settled here at the end of the 17th century after the Spanish crushed the Pueblo Revolt in 1680. The San José mission dates from 1705. Set on the top of the mesa, the Acoma Pueblo, nicknamed "Sky City", is one of the oldest in New Mexico. Its first inhabitants chose this spot more than eight centuries ago, maybe even more if the legends are to be believed. Most of the inhabitants now live in the new village below the old one, where they go to celebrate their festivals. From the Visitor Center, which houses a museum, you can take a guided tour of the village. You can watch the numerous potters plying their craft or visit the mission of San Esteban del Rey, founded at the beginning of the 17th century.

Further west, just before the Arizona border, Gallup is a sort of unofficial "capital" of the Navajos, where most of them go to work. Each year, a rodeo and traditional dances are staged during the Intertribal Indian Ceremonial.

To the south, the Zuni reserve is one of the most welcoming. You can take part in the numerous ceremonies provided you don't take photos. The first conquistadors believed this to be one of the seven fabulous cities of Cibola, the mythical Eldorado, but they quickly changed their minds. The pueblo is well known for its delicate jewellery of silver and turquoises. There is also an interesting museum and a 17th-century mission dedicated to Our Lady of Guadalupe.

From Albuquerque to Taos

Before heading north, make a short detour to the Isleta reservation, south of Albuquerque, to see the mission of San Augustín, founded in 1613. Your next stop should be the pueblo of San Felipe, with its beautiful 18th-century church. Further west, the pueblos of Santa Ana and Jemez are, with rare exceptions, closed to visitors. Only Zia, known for its pottery, is accessible. To the north, in the direction of Santa Fe, the mission of Santo Domingo, founded in 1598, is one of the earliest—but the present building only dates from the 19th century. Also known for its pottery, the village has a cultural centre complete with museum.

A few kilometres away, the Cochiti pueblo is a centre for making ceremonial drums. Here you'll find a mission founded in 1628. The Bandelier National Monument was created to protect the Anasazis Indian ruins of the Frijoles ("fried bean") Canyon.

A host of other pueblos lie north of Santa Fe. The inhabitants of Tesuque inhabitants played a key role in the 1680 revolt. Their campground is overlooked by the remarkable Camel Rock. Corn Dances are held in June and November. San Ildefonso was home to Maria Martinez, who revived black pueblo pottery; some of her pieces can be seen in the small museum. Nambé is known for its delightful waterfalls; a ceremonial dance is held at their foot on July 4. In the hills beyond Santa Clara, you can see the Puye Cliff Dwellings, said to be the tribe's ancestral home. San Juan, one of the most authentic pueblos, had the dubious honour of being the first Spanish capital of New Mexico at the end of the 16th century, until it was transferred to Santa Fe. Picuris (San Lorenzo) pueblo, farther north, just before Taos, is one of the smallest; it harbours an interesting museum and a *kiva* (ceremonial chamber).

Mesa Verde

A gigantic plateau 25 km (16 miles) long and 600 m (1,970 ft) high, the Mesa Verde dominates the plains of Cortez in the south of Colorado. The panorama sweeps from the Rocky Mountains in the north to the Arizona Desert in the west. At its southern edge, the plateau is gashed by small canyons. Scores of Anasazi Indian villages—there could be as many as a thousand—huddle in the wide crevasses and under the rocky overhangs, as if sheltering from the wind and the cold.

Mysterious Origins

Very little is known of the original occupants. The oldest constructions date from 600 BC, the most recent from the 13th century, when for some still undetermined reason the villages were abandoned.

The Pueblo Indians probably settled here to escape drought, or perhaps they were being harassed by another tribe. They subsisted by hunting and farming, their fields rising in terraces, or laid out on the plateau above, sometimes several hours away on foot. They reached them by tortuous pathways, in places scarcely more substantial than a few crude steps cut into the sheer sides of the cliffs.

Rites and Culture

The dwellings were built of clay, and each community had a *kiva* or circular vault where they performed various rites, similar to those of the Hopi today. Their culture seems to have been quite advanced: in the 1980s, an archaeologist discovered at Fajada Butte a sophisticated astronomical calendar for predicting the solstices, equinoxes and lunar eclipses.

Troglodyte Villages

At the height of their civilization, the pueblos established veritable fortresses in the cliffs. Behind the Chapin Mesa Museum, devoted to the Anasazi way of life, Spruce Tree House is one of the biggest and best-preserved troglodyte dwellings of the mesa, and the only one that can be seen in winter. The earlier Cliff Palace, however, is unquestionably the most

New Mexico and Colorado

The villages of the Mesa Verde were inhabited until the 13th century.

beautiful. Under a vast canopy of rock, the architectural complex, discovered in 1888 by two cowboys looking for stray cattle, comprises more than 150 rooms, including 23 *kivas*. Some buildings have as many as four storeys and were home to over 200 people. Perfectly sheltered from the elements, Cliff Palace is in a remarkable state of preservation; some walls are painted with fading Anasazi murals.

Around the Site
You walk down to Cliff Palace from the overlook at the summit of the mesa. Don't be discouraged by the steep gradient; the path, partly by ladder, is short and the site well worth the effort. In winter, the paths are closed by snow.

Two loops in the road inside the park allow you to view ruins dating from different periods. The very evocative four-storey Square Tower House clings to the almost vertical walls of Navajo Canyon. Wetherill Mesa, accessible only in summer (by shuttle bus from the parking area on the mesa) also has numerous ruins, including Long House. To visit it, or indeed Cliff Palace and Balcony House, you need a ticket from the Visitor Center. Think of it in advance; in summer the queues can be long.

Durango

Nestling in the foothills of the Rocky Mountains, some 50 km (30 miles) east of the Mesa Verde Park, Durango was founded at the end of the 19th century, with the arrival of the railway. From the famous Diamond Belle saloon in the Strater Hotel, where the waitresses wear fishnet stockings, to its summer rodeos and Western souvenir shops, the town cultivates with great enthusiasm its aura of the Old West. The dusty old frontier town has long since given way to a vibrant commercial centre full of restaurants and tour agencies offering rafting on the nearby rivers, some of them with raging rapids into the bargain.

Silverton Train

A great number of tourists come here to ride the old Silverton Train, pulled by a steam engine, connecting Durango with the mining town of Silverton, 80 km (50 miles) to the north. You travel aboard old wagons dating from 1880. The round-trip allows you about two hours to mooch around Silverton.

Before setting off on your rail journey, or when you get back, call in at the superb Railroad Museum, located in a big warehouse next to the station. Inside is the Rio Grande Southern engine, dating from 1887, and wagons from the same period, including the sumptuous Nomad, which was once the presidential wagon.

Silverton

Reached by road or rail from Durango, this lonely little town is perched at an altitude of 3,000 m (9,843 ft) in a basin surrounded by the snow-capped tips of the San Juan mountains. It developed mainly after 1874, when gold was discovered in the area. Silverton, with its streets of beaten earth, is even prouder of its past than Durango, and strives hard to keep the nostalgia alive. Everything about the town recalls the Western era and the pioneering spirit: Victorian hotels, restaurants decorated in trapper style, saloons with swinging doors, and so on. Mock duels are organized every afternoon near the old station. The County Jail, now a museum, still has some of its old cells on the first floor. A good many miners who tried to pocket a few nuggets on the sly passed through here before being transferred to the penitentiary. Miners who were a little worse for wear usually landed at the bottom of the stairs in the cellar.

To round off your visit, take a short train ride, hard hat firmly on your head, through the narrow galleries of the Old Hundred gold mine. You can even try your hand at panning for gold.

Cultural Notes

Adobe
Used by the Indians, then adopted by the Spanish, adobe is a brick of mud and straw, dried in the sun. Some missions and old Hispanic buildings, as well as the pueblo villages of eastern Arizona and New Mexico, were constructed with this material.

Body-building
Highly aware of health and fitness, not to say obsessed by the body beautiful, California is the Mecca of body-builders. The phenomenon appeared at the beginning of the 1980s, progressively took over the rest of the states and is now a way of life. Go to the beach to see the end result: a weekend at Venice, south of Santa Monica, says it all.

Country & Western
If there is one type of music particularly appropriate to the West, then it must be country and western. It is broadcast all day long on the radio, and there's no escaping it in restaurants, bars and service stations, blaring from open truck windows. Simple in sentiment, it embodies the soul of a people strongly attached to the land. The words tell stories of love and deception, departures to the cities, nostalgia for the ordinary life.

Hispanics
More than 14 million Mexican immigrants have settled in the American Southwest since the end of World War II. The Americans call them and their descendants "Chicanos" or, more recently, "Hispanics". Entire neighbourhoods of Los Angeles and other cities are almost exclusively their province (for example, 80 per cent of the population of Long Beach). Nevertheless, most still live outside the towns and work as *braceros,* or agricultural labourers. In all, more than a third of today's population of California is Hispanic. The derogatory nickname of "wetbacks" refers to the illegal immigrants, an allusion to their clandestine crossing of the Rio Grande.

Rodeo
Embodying the spirit of the Wild West, the biggest rodeos are usually held in summer and attract cowboys from the four corners of the country, if not the world. Some contestants are professionals who follow the shows around America and Canada. The contests involve hanging on for a few moments to the back of an unsaddled bucking bronco or wild bull. The animals are almost always domesticated, but forced to buck by a tight

leather strap fastened round the lower belly. Throwing a lasso requires a particular skill. The best competitors can lasso a calf and tie the regulation three hooves together in less than ten seconds. The horse is trained to keep the rope under tension so that the fallen calf cannot get up again.

If you have the chance to go to the rodeo, do not hesitate for a second—the spectators are just as intriguing as the events. The final of the Indian rodeo which takes place every year in Arizona or New Mexico is particularly exciting: the best Indian cowboys gather here to show off their skills.

Sport

Sport occupies a primordial place in American life. Like the British, Americans take part in sporting activities at school from their earliest years, and the most popular are American football and baseball.

Not to be confused with European football (always referred to as soccer in the United States), American football is more like rugby. The two teams of eleven men are clad in padded clothing from head to foot to help them withstand violent collisions—any player can be brought down, even if he doesn't have the ball.

Baseball is similar to the English game of rounders, with nine players per side. The most exciting moment is when a batter manages a home run, having sent the ball over the outfield fences, 400 ft (122 m) away from home plate. He and any other players on the base each score a run.

Surf

Along the coast of body-conscious California, surfing is the king of sports. At weekends the beaches are thronged with surfers of all ages looking for the perfect wave, even if the breakers are not up to the standards of Hawaii, where the specialists go to train in winter. It usually takes several days of practice just to stay upright on the board—after that, it's up to you!

Western Lifestyle

Although most ranches are now modernized, "Western" life is still experienced on both sides of the Rockies by more than 10,000 real cowboys. The mountainous and often wooded terrain of Arizona and Utah demands the maintenance of this tradition.

Calves are castrated and dehorned at three months during the great spring round-up. Weaned at seven months, they are put out to pasture and fattened until two years old. Today, around 110 million cattle graze the immense American Prairies. The unprecedented increase in beef consumption since World War II, about 55 kg (120 lb) per person per year, has caused a population explosion of the nation's cattle.

Shopping

The United States is truly a paradise for shoppers. The range of goods is amazing, consumer protection laws ensure that customers' interests are paramount, and sales staff have a refreshingly positive attitude. Here the customer is always right. Be prepared for the addition of a local sales tax that varies from 4 to 10 per cent, depending on the state. For special promotions and sales, look in the Friday and Sunday editions of local newspapers, where you'll also find details of the numerous flea markets (swap meets) where bargains are to be found.

Where to Shop

Giant shopping centres or malls, are found in towns, on the outskirts, and in the suburbs. Each one gathers dozens, sometimes hundreds, of different outlets. Department stores, famous-name designer boutiques and speciality shops (sock shops, tie shops, and so on) are enclosed in a climate-controlled space. Not only do you have a vast array of goods to choose from, but also, the sales staff are unfailingly pleasant and polite. And if you're feeling hungry, plenty of eating places are available, too. It's here that most Americans do their shopping.

Flat-woven Navajo blankets in a style known as "eye-dazzler", with diamonds, zigzags and stripes.

Jewellery

Gold in particular is a good bargain in the United States. Most jewellery stores in the malls offer a large choice. You should remember that American gold is 14 carat rather than the 18 carat which is common all over the European Union.

Electronic and Photographic Goods

In the centre of the large cities—near the Convention Center in Los Angeles or Chinatown's Grant Avenue in San Francisco, for example—specialized shops sell goods at almost ridiculous prices, sometimes half the price you would pay in Europe. Bear in mind, however, that audio-visual equipment operates on the NTSC system, incompatible with Pal-

Secam, so that American video cassettes will not function on European machines. On the other hand, audio cassettes and CDs present no problems.

Before buying anything, check the quality and make sure that you are given an international guarantee certificate. Some shops accept only cash or traveller's cheques, and refuse credit cards. A cautionary remark: check with your local Customs and Excise before leaving as to whether or not it is legal to import the equipment you are planning to buy.

In addition to VAT, there is an import tax specific to goods bought in the United States; the rate varies from one country to another.

Clothing

All the well-known American and European labels can be found in the malls and, there again, prices are very reasonable. In addition, the shops here are absolute heaven for those blessed with a "fuller figure", as there is a multitude of big-size clothes in decidedly unfrumpy styles. And the same goes for "petite" sizes.

This is also a good place to invest in sportswear, for the choice is immense. Because of the nation's passion for keeping fit, there are thousands of shops selling leisure clothes, some of them specialized to the extreme: women's tennis wear, for instance, or T-shirts and sweatshirts adorned with the emblems of the most famous football and baseball teams.

Indian Handicrafts

In Arizona, the craftwork tradition is very much alive, producing a wide range of high-quality objects. Even if the price of these hand-made goods is sometimes rather high, you will find it hard to resist buying one or two items as souvenirs.

Silver and turquoise, both of which are widely found and mined in the West, are the raw materials most often used for Indian jewellery. In the region of Monument Valley, stalls are set by the roadside.

You'll also see people selling magnificent Navajo rugs and woollen blankets, woven in vividly coloured geometrical patterns. Pots are decorated with similar designs.

Something easier to carry home is a dreamcatcher, a complicated web to be suspended over your bed to entangle nightmares in its threads. The good dreams find their way through.

The Hopi sell kachina dolls, but remember that these painted wooden figurines are respected symbols of the gods, not just reproductions destined for the tourist trade.

Dining Out

Maybe you think it's incongruous to use the word "cuisine" when talking about American food. You're in for a pleasant surprise. America is a veritable melting-pot of many cultures, and here you have the perfect opportunity to taste specialities from every corner of the earth. Mexican, of course, all over the Southwest and elsewhere; Asian, in every Chinatown, especially on the West Coast; Italian, absolutely everywhere; Kosher, Greek, Polish, German—not forgetting French. Each culture has contributed its best dishes to the gastronomic palette to a point where the Americans themselves have forgotten the origin. Tell them that a pizza comes from Italy, and they probably won't believe you!

Breakfast

A typical American breakfast is something like a British one, but much more copious, featuring both sweet and savoury dishes. It generally includes fried eggs, bacon, sausages, toast, fruit juice and coffee. The coffee is freely available, and as it is typically much weaker than what is found in Europe, you can drink as much as you like without worrying about your nerves. Also on offer are cereals, muffins and pancakes laced with maple syrup. San Francisco is famous for its unleavened sourdough bread.

Salads

Extremely popular in restaurants throughout the country, and especially so in California where everyone spends hours counting calories, salads are typically American in size—gigantic. One is enough for a whole meal. Many restaurants have self-service salad bars, where you can help yourself to as much as you like of the various vegetables and fruit on offer. In other restaurants you may be served a salad automatically with the main dish—it is included in the price. The West Coast has two specialities: Crab Louis, a salad of the much-prized crab, tomatoes and eggs with chilli sauce; and a salad of raw spinach and crispy bacon, with a cream dressing.

The choice of salad dressings is dizzying. The most commonly available are Italian (oil, vinegar and herbs), French (tomato-flavoured), Ranch (with garlic), Blue Cheese (guess!), and Thousand Island (mayonnaise with chopped gherkins and hard-boiled egg).

Meat

There's no denying that American beef is of very good quality. Cheap, full of flavour, tender, it is the staple meat of the American diet. Steaks are so big they almost cover the plate. In steak houses such as Denny's, Sizzler or Shoney's, you can choose the one you fancy. The most popular cut is the T-bone. You can ask for it rare, medium or well done.

The classic American method of cooking meat is to barbecue it on a charcoal grill, in the time-honoured fashion of the cowboy. Beef or pork ribs are very good, a rack of chops cooked to perfection, drenched in spicy sauces and eaten with the fingers.

Tex-Mex food is a less spicy version of Mexican, centred on beef and bean *chilli con carne* and variations of the corn-meal tortilla.

Fish and Seafood

Most steak houses also serve fish dishes, although fish is not really an American speciality. At Fisherman's Wharf in San Francisco, the swordfish is excellent and the fresh tuna delicious. In the Italian quarter, sample *cioppino*, a fish soup. Other specialities of San Francisco are abalone and oysters in various guises: try the ham and oyster omelette. But lobster, transported from the cold waters off Maine in New England, and shrimp are everyone's favourites. Don't be surprised to see dishes that mix meat and seafood: surf and turf is a classic duo in American cooking.

Traditional Meals and Specialities

Easter, Christmas, New Year and Thanksgiving are occasions for a festive meal, when all the family tries to gather together to enjoy a traditional menu.

Thanksgiving, the last Thursday in November, is the annual commemoration of the first harvest, in 1621, of the Pilgrim Fathers, who had arrived on the shores of the continent the previous year and suffered a winter of great hardship and near starvation. Theirs was the first colony to survive. The Thanksgiving meal is a gargantuan feast: roast stuffed turkey and gravy with cranberry sauce, potatoes, green vegetables and salads and on and on—rather like a traditional British Christmas dinner. The settlers were introduced to cranberries by the Indians, and they helped to combat malnutrition.

Simple yet tasty, hot grilled corn on the cob.

Cheese and Desserts

American cheeses are patterned after European ones, copies of Cheddar, Emmental, and so on—mostly the hard varieties. They are consumed more frequently in a sandwich than as a separate course at the end of a meal. California's speciality is Monterey Jack. You occasionally find some Brie or Camembert imported from France. The orange substance called American Cheese is processed from a variety of milk products and finds its way into grilled sandwiches and cheeseburgers.

If the cheese disappoints, the Americans really excel with their desserts. Beneath the California sun, fruit really does seem to grow bigger, sweeter and juicier than anywhere else, and it is delicious on its own or incorporated into all sorts of cakes, pies, tarts and mousses. Strawberries, peaches and grapefruit are the best. Apple pie is regarded as a classic American dish (with ice cream), but boysenberry pie has its devotees, too, especially around Anaheim, where the hybrid berry was first produced.

The ice cream, in a thousand and one imaginative flavours and shamefully rich, is not to be missed. If you want to go over the top, order a sundae: several scoops of ice cream topped with caramel, strawberry or chocolate syrup, and sprinkled with walnuts or peanuts. A milk shake is a must in the ice cream department: meltingly rich and creamy, they are bursting with calories.

Drinks

You will be surprised by the wide range of soft drinks on offer, Coke and Pepsi being only the tip of the iceberg. Iced tea, fruit juices and vegetable juices are all available, and it is no longer difficult to find bottled mineral water. It is the custom to serve diners automatically a glass of iced tap water as soon as they sit down.

You must be 21 or over to buy alcoholic drinks, or to consume them in public. The selection of wines is as wide as you might find anywhere: imports from all over the world compete with the products of several American states. But at least 80 per cent of the vineyards are in California, so take advantage of your time here to get to know the local vintages. The custom is to identify wine by the grape variety or combination of varieties used: Cabernet Sauvignon, Pinot Noir and Zinfandel, for example, in the reds; Sauvignon Blanc and Chardonnay in the whites. Rosé wines are often called "blush". The Napa and Sonoma valleys near San Francisco produce several first-rate vintages.

American beers are becoming more varied, with the growth of local brands and a fashion for micro-breweries. Domestic or imported beer is always served ice cold. Spirits (called liquor) are normally served with loads of ice, whether "on the rocks" or accompanied by a mixer.

A final note: bar staff expect to be tipped.

Remarks

- In the United States you can eat at any time of the day. You will rarely be refused service.
- Weekends are the time to try brunch in one of the many hotels which offer it. There is always a gigantic buffet which operates on a help-yourself basis.
- If you have been served more than you can cope with on the spot, you can always ask to take away the leftovers of your meal in the famous American "doggy bag"—whether you have a doggy or not.
- You're dying of hunger and feeling so feeble your legs won't carry you another step? Wheel into a drive-through and eat without leaving your car.
- Finally, if you can't be bothered to go out, look in the Yellow Pages and have your favourite pizza or Chinese meal delivered right to your hotel room.

Sports

In this country where sport is a national obsession, there's no place for the idle. The infrastructure is installed for every sport you can imagine—and some which perhaps you never even dreamed of.

Getting Wet

The southern coast of California is excellent for swimming. On most beaches you can enjoy windsurfing or waterskiing. As you'll remember from Beach Boys days, the breakers are great for surfing.

If you like deep-sea fishing, arrangements can be made in Sausalito near San Francisco, Marina del Rey at Los Angeles, and especially San Diego where the sheltered bay is a paradise for yachtsmen.

Diving is particularly pleasant along the rocky coasts, where the beautiful underwater kelp forests serve as playgrounds for seals, sea otters and sea lions.

Keeping Dry

You don't have to get your hair wet to enjoy the beach. Join the jogging hordes, or get on a bike: there are plenty of cycle tracks as cycling is an up-and-coming pastime. You can hire any equipment you need at the resorts. For a feel of the California way of life, get your skates on (rent them at Venice Beach). A skating path follows the coast north to Santa Monica and beyond, and to the south as far as Redondo Beach, in all more than 25 km (16 miles).

Golf

The number of golf courses in the region is staggering and green fees are moderate, so don't hesitate to pack your golf clubs. The courses are very well laid out and attractively landscaped. The best are to be found around Monterey, south of San Francisco, with a wide choice of courses.

Tennis

Tennis is played everywhere, at the hotels or on public courts, some of which are free. It's a good idea to get up early and take advantage of the cool morning air, as after 11 a.m. the heat becomes overwhelming.

In the Mountains

All the national parks and monuments in the West are criss-

Hiking through the beautiful Yosemite National Park.

crossed by well-marked hiking trails. Information is available from the Visitor Centers. Every category is catered for, from the easy half-hour stroll to a trek of several weeks (inform someone of your itinerary). The best place for rock climbing is Yosemite Park.

If you yearn to gallop on horseback across the wide open spaces, go to Monument Valley, where a Navajo guide will show you his territory. Yosemite and Sequoia also cater to the horse-lover.

For winter sports, the Rockies provide a vast snowy playground. In the Sierra Nevada, the chief resorts are Mammoth Lakes and Squaw Valley; here you can leap off your skis and into your skates or your snowmobile. Every western state has its own winter resorts: Alta in Utah; Aspen, Vail and Steamboat in Colorado; Santa Fe and Taos in New Mexico; Fairfield in Arizona.

Spectator Sports

The truly national games are baseball and American football, closely followed by basketball and ice hockey. For atmosphere, nothing can beat a Trojans match (the football team of L.A.'s University of Southern California), or the great annual final of the Super Bowl.

The Hard Facts

Airports

Most international flights to the American West land in Los Angeles (the third-busiest airport in the world in terms of traffic volume) or San Francisco. Alternatively, your itinerary may land you at Albuquerque, Phoenix or Las Vegas. In fact, practically every city in the United States has its own airport.

Los Angeles International Airport (LAX), on Santa Monica Bay, is 24 km (15 miles) from the centre. Trains and coaches are available to central and surrounding areas.

San Francisco International Airport (SFO) is 25 km (15 miles) southeast of the city. Airporter buses run every 20 minutes from 5 a.m.–11 p.m. Limousine, taxi and public buses are also available.

Oakland International Airport (OAK) is 32 km (20 miles) from San Francisco, across the bay. Air-BART buses connect with the BART rapid transit system to central San Francisco.

San Diego International Airport (SAN) is 5 km (3 miles) west of the city. It mainly receives domestic traffic.

McCarran International Airport (LAS) is 8 km (5 miles) from central Las Vegas. Routes 108 and 109 of the CTA bus service have direct access to the airport, with a stop directly outside the baggage claim area, on Level Zero.

Salt Lake City International Airport (SLC) is close to the centre. An airport bus runs every 60 minutes.

Phoenix Sky Harbor International Airport (PHX) is 6 km (4 miles) from the city centre. A bus service to the centre runs every 25 minutes from 6 a.m. to 6.20 p.m. Taxis are available 24 hours a day.

Albuquerque International Sunport (ABQ) is 6 km (4 miles) southeast of the city centre. A bus operates every 20 minutes between 7.03 a.m. and 6.13 p.m.; there are several shuttle buses, and taxis are available.

The biggest airports have car-hire agencies, a tourist office, banks, shops, a post office, restaurants and, where appropriate, free shuttle bus services to other terminals, the principal hotels, and to the parking lots of car-hire firms. If you have a lot of luggage, you will always find a porter or a trolley (keep some 25¢ coins handy or purchase a ticket from a machine).

Climate

The vast extent of the territory means that the climate varies from place to place in the West. California alone, because of its size, covers several climatic zones. The climate of the entire Pacific coast is mild. All year round, the south coast basks happily in a Mediterranean-type warmth which becomes increasingly torrid as you approach the Mojave Desert. Summers there are extremely hot (temperatures of 40°C, or 104°F, are not at all uncommon). The winters, with a few scattered showers, are mild and sunny. At some places in southern California you can quickly pass from sea to desert or from snow to orange groves.

Northern California enjoys a much cooler, more humid climate. Winter in San Francisco is comparable to winter by the sea in Western Europe. Even in summer, the temperature rarely rises above 20°C (68°F), and evening fogs are frequent. Smog is a problem during hot weather, especially in Los Angeles from June until August. Away from the coast, the Sierra Nevada, Utah and to a lesser extent the north of Arizona experience snowfalls in autumn which are sufficiently heavy to close certain roads until spring.

Just in case you have gone thoroughly metric—the Americans have not—here is a formula for converting Fahrenheit to Centigrade. Subtract 32, divide by 9, multiply by 5, and there you have it. For a rough guide, 20°C = 68°F, 30°C = 86°F, and 40°C = 104°F. Water boils at 212°F and freezes at 32°F.

Communications

Post offices are open between 9 a.m. and 5 p.m. non-stop, sometimes later still in the large towns. They handle letters and parcels only. To send a telegram you have to contact a private company (Western Union) which has representatives in the supermarkets. The price of a letter to Europe depends of course on its weight, but the minimum charge is 90¢, the same for a postcard. Deliveries take 4 to 6 days on average, but an express service guarantees arrival in 24 to 48 hours. If you cannot find a post office, stamps are widely available (with a surcharge) from automatic distributors in hotels, drugstores, airports, etc. Fax facilities are common, and every hotel will fax documents for you for a modest sum.

To telephone from a public phone box, you can buy a call card (issued by a host of private companies); otherwise keep a supply of 25¢ coins handy. To place a call to anywhere in the United States, dial 1 (for long-distance), plus the three-digit local area code, plus the number. An operator will ask you to insert coins for a three-minute call, and will ask for additional coins if you stay on the line for more than three minutes. The procedure is the same to place a call abroad: dial 011 (international), 44 (for Britain for example), your correspondent's area code (minus the initial zero) and number. If you have an international charge card, it will save you much wrestling with coins.

Consulates

Embassies are located in Washington DC, but many countries additionally maintain consulates in the principal cities. Should you have a problem with the local authorities or lose your travel documents or money, this is the place to go. You'll find them listed under "Consulates" in the telephone directory.

Driving

American roads are in general excellent. Highways link all the large towns, and dual carriageways are widespread. On a few private turnpikes and bridges there is a toll charge. You will soon notice that Americans jump into their car at the drop of a hat. This is possibly because of the ridiculously low price of petrol, at least until recently—it has now risen to more than $3 per gallon. Petrol is unleaded or diesel.

Speed limits are lower than in Europe at 55 or 65 mph (90–105 kph) on the highways (motorways), 55 mph (90 kph) on other main roads and 25 to 35 mph (40–55 kph) in built-up areas. The police are very much in evidence and use the latest equipment to enforce the speed limits strictly. Parking is controlled: be careful or your car could be towed away! It is a serious offence to drink and drive; even to carry an open container of alcohol in the car is illegal. Seat belts are obligatory everywhere.

If you arrive at a junction at the same time as another car, then the car on the right has priority; otherwise cars cross alternately after a pause. Two flashing red lights are equivalent to a stop sign. In the absence of any indication to the contrary, you can turn right at a red light after first coming to a brief halt.

Be very careful if you see one of the yellow school buses. If it is stationary with its rotating light switched on, then you must on no account overtake it from either direction.

To help you find your way around, road maps are available free from tourist offices. Directions are given by route numbers rather than by the name of the destination. In the large cities, traffic congestion is often a serious problem, so avoid the rush hours if possible.

Electricity
The domestic electrical supply is 110 volts, 60 cycles AC. Sockets are for plugs with two flat pins. If you are planning to use electrical equipment (a razor, for example), then buy an adaptor or even a transformer before leaving home.

Emergencies
Whatever the emergency, dial 911. The operator will put you in touch with the police, fire brigade or medical services as required.

Essentials
Rest assured; anything which you may have forgotten will be available where you are. Virtually the only exception is medication. If you are following a course of treatment, take your medicines with you to avoid having to change brand or dosage.

If you are travelling in summer take light clothing, with a sweater for the evenings. Remember that the American style is very casual. In winter, spring or autumn, dress as you would in Europe. Whatever else, remember to pack your bathing costume!

Formalities
Citizens of the European Union with machine-readable passports or biometric passports do not need a visa to visit the United States for a stay of three months maximum. In principle, passports must be valid for 6 months beyond the date of departure from the US. You may require a visa to cross into Canada or Mexico. Check with your travel agent well before your departure. Children must have their own passports. Check with your travel agent or the American embassy beforehand.

During the flight you will be given a customs declaration form to fill in. It is very simple: you have to declare gifts exceeding a total of $100 in value, and both cash and travellers cheques exceeding $10,000. Personal possessions are exempt from tax. In addition, each adult can import 1 litre of alcohol, and 200 cigarettes or 50 cigars.

Fruit, vegetables and meats may not be imported—eat them or dispose of them before arrival in the bins provided before customs. Sniffer dogs are on duty to locate drugs, but food can interest them, too.

Upon arrival, all visitors between 14 and 79 are fingerprinted and photographed.

Health
Medical treatment, especially hospital care, is very expensive. Americans who can afford to do

so take out private medical insurance. It is imperative that you are insured before leaving home; check that your policy covers the United States. Holiday insurance specialists can recommend policies which give complete coverage in the event of accident or illness.

Having said that, remember to take the obvious precautions of using a sun cream with a high protection factor (at least 20) and wearing a hat, for the most dangerous thing is the sun. Be aware of the possibility of dehydration and drink lots of water in very hot weather.

Holidays and festivals
Shops and offices are closed on the following days:

January 1	New Year's Day
Third Mon. in January	Martin Luther King Day
Third Mon. in February	Presidents Day
Last Mon. in May	Memorial Day
July 4	Independence Day
First Mon. in September	Labor Day
Second Mon. in October	Columbus Day
November 11	Veterans' Day
Fourth Thurs. in November	Thanksgiving
December 25	Christmas Day
Moveable:	Easter Monday

Language
A few words differ between British and American English, but nothing should present an insurmountable problem. The English word "pavement" means the roadway to Americans, who use sidewalk. A banknote is a bill in the States, a restaurant bill is called a check or a tab, a handbag becomes a purse and the ground floor of a building is called the first floor. A lift is an elevator, a subway an underpass, the underground train is the subway. Parts of the car (automobile) have different names, too: the handbrake is called a parking brake; the boot is the trunk, the bonnet is the hood and the windscreen a windshield.

The Americans often use contractions for signs and sometimes you may have to think a bit; for example the strange Ped Xing is a shortened version of "pedestrian crossing".

Media
The American press is decentralized. Every state, indeed every town, has its own newspapers, tending to focus on local news. In California, *The Los Angeles Times* and *The San Francisco Examiner* are the two leading daily newspapers. The Sunday papers have countless different sections (Entertainment, Travel, Books, etc. are mines of informa-

tion) and a copy can weigh several pounds and take you a month to read! There are very few national daily papers apart from *USA Today* and *The New York Times* (*The Wall Street Journal* for financial news).

Similarly, radio and television broadcasting is regional. There are more than 7,000 radio stations and 1,000 television channels, but only a handful of national broadcasters (ABC, CBS, NBC). Of the hundreds of cable TV channels, the best known are MTV (music), CNN (non-stop news) and HBO (cinema).

Money

The unit of currency is the dollar ($), which is divided into 100 cents (¢). There are 1, 5, 10, 50 and 100 dollar notes (bills), all of the same size and colour, so beware! New $20, $50 and $100 banknotes are in circulation along with the old; other denominations will gradually follow. Two-dollar notes, commemorating the Bicentenary of American Independence, and $1,000 notes are rare.

The four main coins are the penny (1¢), the nickel (5¢), the dime (10¢) and the quarter (25¢). Other rare coins in circulation are the half-dollar (50¢) and dollar, the latter found almost exclusively in casinos.

It is difficult to change currency in the United States anywhere other than at the major airports. It is better to buy your dollars before departure or to withdraw them on the spot from cashpoint machines using a credit card. (Visa and Mastercard are accepted everywhere). Travellers cheques in dollars can be used like cash, with change always given.

National Parks

To drive through a national park you have to pay a fee of $10–20. If you wish to visit several parks, or the same one several times, it is worth investing in a National Parks Pass, valid one year, for $50.

Opening Hours

Working hours are normally from 9 a.m. to 6 p.m. Shops always stay open during the lunch hour. In the malls, shops are often open until late in the evening and, what's more, generally open on Sundays (except for Mormon Utah). Supermarkets and local foodstores often stay open 24 hours per day and seven days per week. The banks form the exception which proves the rule, having opening hours restricted to 10 a.m. until 3 p.m., and until 5 or 6 p.m. on Fridays.

Religion

Religion plays a very important role in the United States where more than one American in two is a regular churchgoer. The numerous Protestant faiths include Baptist, Methodist and Presbyterian, which have the largest memberships. Some Churches insist on a rigorous interpretation of the Bible. Catholics are fewer in number, but nevertheless total more than 50 million. Many other religions and sects are represented as well.

If you would like to attend a service, consult the Yellow Pages, which list all faiths in alphabetical order.

If you have the opportunity, step inside the magnificent Los Angeles glass cathedral, for a look around.

Security

Contrary to popular belief, the United States is a relatively safe country, provided you stay away from the insalubrious areas of large cities. Take sensible measures in the large towns and on certain beaches: do not walk around late at night, especially not alone; leave your passport and valuables in the hotel safe; leave nothing open to view in your car.

Time Zones

The continental United States is divided into four time zones. The frontier of Arizona marks the change from Pacific Time (California) to Mountain Time (the Wild West). In summer the clocks are put forward an hour for Daylight Saving Time; consequently California is 8 hours behind Britain all year round. Noon in Los Angeles is equivalent to 8 p.m. in London. Phoenix is only 7 hours behind Britain. The Navajo Reservation has its own summer time.

Tipping

In the United States, many people are paid for their work exclusively by tips. In bars and restaurants, the norm for gratuities is a minimum of 15 per cent of the bill, 20 per cent if you wish to express particular satisfaction. Taxi drivers and tour guides expect a similar tip. Give porters $1 per bag, guides and chambermaids $1 or $2 per day of your stay.

Toilets

You will find toilets (restrooms) in airports, railway and bus stations, large stores and petrol (gas) stations (you may need to ask for the key). Restaurants (including fast food establishments) reserve their facilities for their clients. Toilets are always free.

Tourist Offices

Every state has its tourist office which publishes maps and brochures of excellent quality. These are available in the Welcome Centers situated on the main highways, generally at the state boundary, or in the large towns. The Convention and Visitors Bureau provides local information.

Transport

Americans usually fly from one large town to another. Airlines serve practically all towns, even relatively small ones. Trains, although very comfortable, even luxurious, are not very efficient as there are relatively few routes. Besides, the cost of rail travel is often as high as flying.

Long-distance bus routes are very competitively priced, and dominated by the Greyhound company, serving most of the country except for the national parks. But journeys can take days.

For shorter distances, the best solution is to hire a car. Without one, in fact, it's difficult to go anywhere. The minimum age requirement for care hire is often 25; where it is as low as 21, a daily surcharge of $5 or $10 is imposed, depending on the state and the rental company. A European driving licence is accepted as well as an international licence. Rental charges are attractive and usually include unlimited mileage. Remember to ask if the cost includes insurance, for which there are various options.

The other solution for short distances is the taxi. In Los Angeles they stop only at taxi ranks. Local public transport in the West, as everywhere else in the country, is thin on the ground. Buses are infrequent. Los Angeles and San Francisco both have clean and convenient underground railways (subways). In central San Francisco, the main sites are served by cable cars.

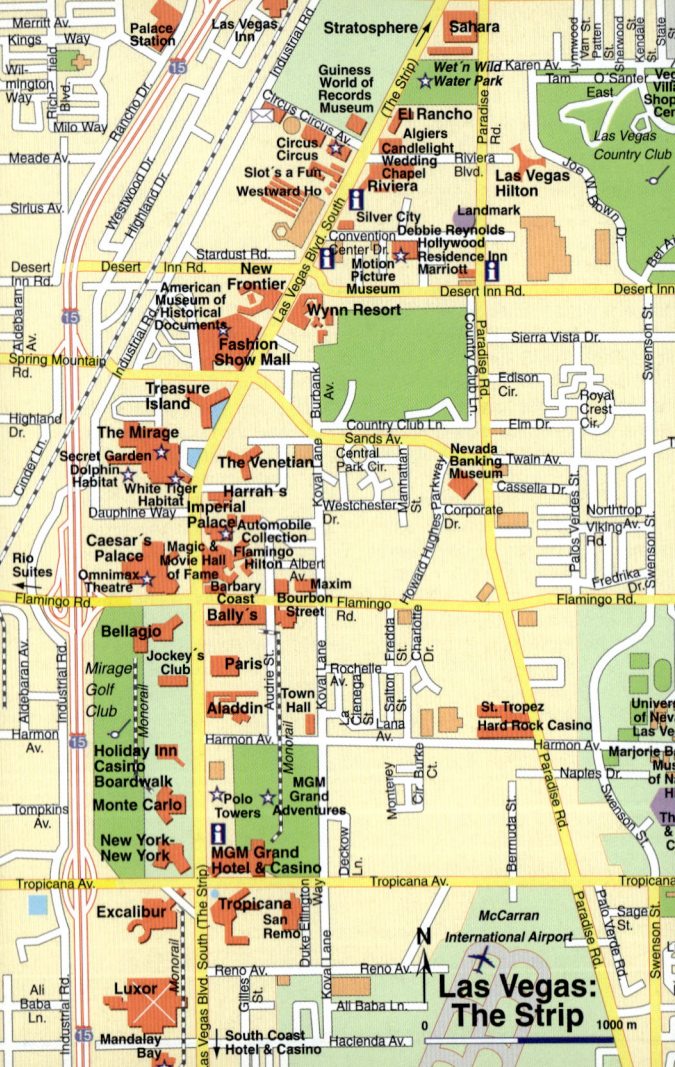

INDEX

Albuquerque 79–80
Alcatraz 24
Anaheim 46–47
Antelope Canyon 68
Anza Borrego 51
Arches NP 60–61
Berkeley 26
Beverly Hills 45
Big Sur 30
Biosphere-2 75
Bisbee 77
Bodie 38
Bryce Canyon 59–60
California Desert 50–53
Camino Real 30
Canyonlands 61–62
Capitol Reef NP 60
Carmel 29–30
Channel Islands 34–35
Chelly Canyon 65
Death Valley 53
Disneyland Resort 46–47
Durango 89
Flagstaff 72–73
Ghost Towns 77
Goosenecks 60
Grand Canyon 68–72
Great Salt Lake 62
Havasupai 72
Hearst Castle 31–33
Hollywood 43–44
Indian Corner 63–64
Indian pueblos 84–87
Joshua Tree 53
Kings Canyon NP 38
Las Vegas 54–56
Lompoc Valley 33
Los Angeles 41–47
Malibu 46
Mammoth Lakes 37–38
Marble Canyon 68
Mesa Verde 87–88
Meteorite Crater 66
Mono, Lake 38
Monterey 29
Montezuma Castle 73
Monument Valley 63–64
Muir Woods 27
Napa Valley 27
Navajo Monument 64–65
Oak Creek Canyon 72
Organ Pipe 76
Page 66
Palm Springs 51–53
Pasadena 42–43
Petrified Forest 65–66
Phoenix 73–74
Point Lobos 30
Point Reyes 27
Powell, Lake 66
Prescott 74
Saguaro National Monument 75–76
Salt Lake City 62
San Diego 49–50
San Francisco 15–27
San Xavier Mission 75
Santa Barbara 33–35
Santa Fe 80–83
Santa Monica 46
Sausalito 26
Scottsdale 73–74
Sedona 72–73
Sequoia NP 38
Silverton 89
Skywalk 72
Slot canyons 68
Solvang 34
Sonoma Valley 27
Taos 83–84
Tombstone 77
Tucson 74–76
Yosemite NP 37
Zion NP 59

GENERAL EDITOR
Barbara Ender-Jones
ENGLISH ADAPTATION
J. Farr, C. Grisewood
LAYOUT
Luc Malherbe
PHOTO CREDITS
Claude Hervé-Bazin
Seide Preis: p. 2
hemis.fr/Houze: p. 14;
/Renault: p. 40; /Frumm:
pp. 44, 92; /Wysocki: p. 71;
/Frilet: p. 78;
Kurt Ohlhoff: p. 32
istockphoto.com/Eilers:
p. 48; /Prott: p. 61;
/Luchschen: p. 74;
/Belton: p. 97;
/Rasmussen: p. 99;
/Falk: p. 101
Georges Herzog: p. 58
MAPS
JPM Publications

Copyright © 2008, 1997
by JPM Publications S.A.
12, avenue William-Fraisse,
1006 Lausanne, Switzerland
information@jpmguides.com
http://www.jpmguides.com/

All rights reserved. No part of this book may be reproduced or transmitted in any form or by any means, electronic or mechanical, including photocopying, recording or by any information storage and retrieval system without permission in writing from the publisher.
Every care has been taken to verify the information in the guide, but neither the publisher nor his client can accept responsibility for any errors that may have occurred. If you spot an inaccuracy or a serious omission, please let us know.

Printed in Switzerland
Weber/Bienne – 10208.00.3572
Edition 2008